RESCUING JESUS
from the CHRISTIANS

RESCUING JESUS
from the CHRISTIANS

CLAYTON SULLIVAN

TRINITY PRESS INTERNATIONAL
Harrisburg, Pennsylvania

Trinity Press International, P.O. Box 1321, Harrisburg, PA 17105

Trinity Press International is a division of The Morehouse Group.

Cover design: Laurie Westhafer

Library of Congress Cataloging-in-Publication Data

Sullivan, Clayton, 1930-
    Rescuing Jesus from the Christians / Clayton Sullivan.
      p. cm.
    Includes bibliographical references and index.
    ISBN 1-56338-380-2 (alk. paper)
    1. Jesus Christ – Historicity. 2. Jesus Christ – Teachings. I. Title.

  BT301.3 .S85 2002
  232.9'08 – dc21

                            2001052457

Printed in the United States of America

02   03   04   05   06   07   10 9 8 7 6 5 4 3 2 1

For Clayton, Elisabeth, and Taylor

Contents

Preface

Rescuing Jesus from the Christians has not been written for academics or for the clergy. Instead, it has been written for reflective laypersons who are not satisfied with the belief system they encounter in orthodox Christianity. I have written *Rescuing Jesus from the Christians* out of the conviction we are living in an era that requires a reconceptualization of the Christian faith. I hope this small book contributes to that end. Because of this book's lay orientation, I have provided a glossary that defines many of the terms (like "Synoptic Gospels" and "pantheism") used on the pages that follow.

I express gratitude to Sarah Waddle for bibliographic assistance, and I express gratitude to Mercer University Press for permission to use data published in my book *Rethinking Realized Eschatology.* I also express gratitude to Laura Hudson and Henry Carrigan of Trinity Press for their editorial assistance. Most of all, I wish to express thanks to Beverly J. Davis, computer specialist par excellence. She has patiently typed and retyped the text of this book as it has undergone numerous revisions. *Rescuing Jesus from the Christians* would never have been published without her able assistance.

Biblical quotations are from the Revised Standard Version. However, three passages (Matthew 15:21–28, Mark 12:18–25, and Luke 16:19–31) are from the New English Bible, and one passage (Luke 19:38) is from the New Revised Standard Version.

Part One

The Recovery of the Historical Jesus

Few people have lived about whom it can be said, "they changed the course of human history." These words can be spoken of Alexander the Great and Muhammad. We can also say this about Jesus of Nazareth, the Jewish prophet whose teachings and followers launched Christianity. Today some two billion Christians around the world view him as an authentic religious teacher. They refer to him as "Lord" and "Savior" and "Son of God." He is also held in esteem by a billion Muslims.

Many of these admirers, however, are unaware that for the past two hundred years scholars have subjected Jesus' earthly life to meticulous and detailed examination. And they are unaware of many of the conclusions of this thorough study. This unawareness is not surprising because for centuries no one either inside or outside the church paid particular attention to the human, earthly life Jesus lived as a Jew on the eastern frontier of the Roman Empire. Instead, orthodox Christianity viewed, and continues to view, Jesus as a mysterious, other-worldly person to be encountered in hymns and anthems, in creeds and dogmas, in icons and stained-glass windows, and in porcelain Christo-statues displayed in ecclesiastical art stores in Boston and New York.

To express this matter another way, Christians have tended across the years to view Jesus through theological or dogmatic spectacles, not through historical spectacles. Theologians have

1

expended mental-speculative energy hammering out the Trinitarian Dogma. They have pondered: What was the significance of Jesus' death? How did both a divine and human nature coexist within him? How does one explain the incarnation? Prolonged attention to these kinds of questions led to Jesus becoming ensconced in a creedal castle. Theologians who constructed this castle were well intentioned, and for centuries their beliefs about Jesus were accepted without question. In the second part of this book, however, I shall contend that some of these beliefs have experienced a depletion of plausibility and have become obsolete. Hence the need exists to rescue Jesus from a creedal prison consisting of beliefs that no longer make sense to a lot of people.

This rescuing or reassessment is necessary because approximately two hundred years ago a mutation took place in Christian thought, a mutation that was a by-product of the Enlightenment. Instead of further elaborating the Jesus of dogma, numerous thinkers began a quest for the historical Jesus, the human Jesus of flesh and blood who was a prophet in Galilee and who was crucified by Pilate. They sought a straightforward, unvarnished account of Jesus' earthly life as it was prior to its being smothered in dogmatic speculations created by an admiring church. Before the Enlightenment, scholars thought Jesus' life was "too holy" or "too sacred" to be studied in the same way they might study the life of Napoleon or Charlemagne or Henry VIII. To study Jesus' life in this manner would be an act of irreverence. Thus the Enlightenment's decision to search for the historical Jesus was comparable to a late fifteenth-century nautical voyage of discovery. It was a new departure — the setting out on a course never sailed before. This search for the historical Jesus was begun by Hermann Samuel Reimarus, an obscure German scholar who was a professor of oriental languages in Hamburg and who died in 1768. His studies were posthumously published by G. E. Lessing — a librarian, philosopher, and theologian — in a collection of writings entitled the *Wolfenbüttel Fragments*. One of Reimarus's essays in this anthology was entitled "On the Intentions of Jesus and His Disciples." Before Reimarus, no one had attempted to formulate a historical understanding of Jesus' life. Reimarus, by contrast, treated the Gospels as historical documents and endeavored to place the events and ideas recorded in them in a historical context. Subsequently other scholars have walked in Reimarus's footsteps. Indeed, throughout the nineteenth and twentieth centuries scores of lives of Jesus were written by scholars who grappled with such questions as: What was the historical, geographical, and ideological setting of Jesus' life? What message did Jesus proclaim to his contemporaries? What was his intention? What did he accomplish? What happened to him?

This search for the historical Jesus, rather than the Jesus of hymns and creeds, has been a long and complex enterprise.[1] Having begun in the eighteenth century, the quest continues to the present. To be sure, some of the earliest lives of Jesus were speculative. Engaging in conjecture, they tried to do the impossible by seeking to trace Jesus' inner psychological and spiritual development. They sought to discover the "real" Jesus "behind" the Jesus portrayed in the four gospels.[2] Granting that false starts were made, out of this two-century quest a number of questions were raised that the church had previously ignored. Some of these questions are problematic or puzzling and have never been answered to everyone's satisfaction.

On the pages that follow I shall give attention to several of these questions. I have no intention of attempting to write a life of Jesus; superb lives of Jesus have been written.[3] Nor do I intend to discuss matters over which disagreements do not exist. For example, no one disputes that Jesus told parables, observed Passover, held the law of Moses in esteem, and was crucified outside Jerusalem. Instead, I intend to discuss controversial-problematic questions over which well-intentioned people can disagree. Some of the controversial questions include: What was the main message Jesus delivered to his Jewish contemporaries? What was his attitude toward non-Jews? What circumstances surrounded his birth? Did Jesus believe he was God? What about his ethical teachings? Why was he crucified by the Romans?

These questions go a long way toward helping us understand the historical Jesus.[4] Later in this book I shall contend that the Christian faith has nothing to fear from these queries or from answers given to them by post-Enlightenment research.

I suggest we begin by grappling with the following issue: What was the main message Jesus proclaimed to his fellow Jews? What gospel did he preach? I shall give extensive attention to this query. Jesus' major message cannot be explained in one or two sentences. Moreover, the answer one gives to this query significantly influences a person's understanding and evaluation of the historical Jesus. Was Jesus' major message true? Or was it a mistake? Was his central message authentic? Or was it erroneous? There are two answers to these questions: (1) The kingdom of God was Jesus' major message. He believed and taught that a magnificent kingdom for Jews was to arrive on this earth during the lifetime of his contemporaries. (2) This kingdom did not appear. Thus Jesus' preaching ministry concerning the kingdom of God was predicated on a mistake.

Notes

1. The classic survey of opening decades of the search for the "historical Jesus" is the book by Albert Schweitzer translated into English under the title *The Quest of the Historical Jesus* (London: A. and C. Black, 1954, repr., London: SCM Press, 1981. Schweitzer's book was published originally in German under the title *Von Reimarus zu Wrede*. Of superb value is a book edited by Gregory W. Dawes entitled *The Historical Jesus Quest* (Louisville: Westminster John Knox Press, 1999). This book discusses scholars who have played a pivotal role in the historical Jesus quest: Hermann Samuel Reimarus, David Friedrich Strauss, William Wrede, Johannes Weiss, to mention a few, and excerpts from their major works are given.

2. A critique of these earlier lives of Jesus is found in Martin Kähler, *The So-Called Historical Jesus and the Historic Biblical Christ* (Philadelphia: Fortress, 1964). This book was originally published in German in 1896. In this book Kähler asserted "the Jesus of the 'Life-of-Jesus movement' is merely a modern example of human creativity, and (is) not one iota better than the notorious dogmatic Christ of Byzantine Christology" (p. 43). He also quipped, "I regard the entire Life-of-Jesus movement as a blind alley" (p. 46).

3. No words exist in the English language to praise adequately Professor E. P. Sanders's book entitled *The Historical Figure of Jesus* (London: Penguin

Books, 1993). This work encapsulates contemporary New Testament scholarship at its best. Every person interested in understanding Jesus' life from a historical viewpoint should read Professor Sanders's book. Also of superb value is Paula Fredriksen, *Jesus of Nazareth: King of the Jews* (New York: Vintage Books, 2000). Neither of these books is an "easy" read. They require concentration.

4. Writing a historical account of Jesus' life is a problematic task. Students of the New Testament do not know precisely *when* the Gospels were written. They do not know *where* or *by whom* they were written. There is no agreement on what weight should be assigned noncanonical gospels like the Gospel of Thomas. The New Testament gospels contain fanciful particulars (like the star that appeared in the sky at the time of Jesus' birth). Jesus' life as presented in the Fourth Gospel is vastly different from Jesus' life as presented in the first three gospels. Moreover, the Jesus materials in the Gospels are contradictory. Consider, for example, the question of who was present when the women arrived at Jesus' empty tomb after the resurrection. Mark says a young man was present when the women arrived at the tomb. Matthew says an angel was present while Luke says two men were there. They were dressed in dazzling clothes. The Fourth Gospel reports two angels were present. Such contradictions abound. Their presence demonstrates the futility of defending the viewpoint that the Bible is an infallible or consistent document.

Chapter 1

What Was Jesus'
Main Message?

Out of the two-hundred-year search for the historical Jesus, investigators concluded his dominant message was: The kingdom of God is soon to arrive on earth. Its appearance is just around the corner. Indeed, the kingdom's imminent arrival constituted the original gospel.[1] Thus Mark's gospel epitomizes Jesus' major message as follows: "The time is fulfilled, and the kingdom of God is at hand; repent and believe in the gospel" (Mark 1:14–15). John Reumann was on target when he wrote, "Ask any hundred New Testament scholars around the world, Protestant, Catholic, or non-Christian, what the central message of Jesus of Nazareth was, and the vast majority of them — perhaps every single expert — would agree that this message centered in the 'Kingdom of God.'"[2]

This is all well and good. No one disputes the centrality of the kingdom in Jesus' teachings. But curiously enough, students of his thought have never agreed on what he meant by "Kingdom of God." Across the years this phrase has been a verbal Rorschach inkblot. It has been semantic putty — pulled, shaped, and squeezed in all directions. Some interpreters have identified the kingdom with "heaven" and a blessed future life. Others have equated the kingdom with a curative power operative or realized in Jesus' healings.[3] Social reformers have contended the kingdom is a just social order.[4] Adolf von Harnack defined the kingdom as the rule of the Holy God in human hearts.[5] Immanuel Kant defined the kingdom as "the gradual transition of ecclesiastical faith to the exclusive sovereignty of pure religious faith"[6] while Stephen Mitchell defined the kingdom as "a state of being, a way of living at ease among the joys and sorrows of *our* world"; it is "feeling, as if we were floating in the womb of the universe, that we are being taken care of at every moment."[7] Roman Catholic theologians, as the 1994 *Catechism of the Catholic Church* states, insist the kingdom is the church.[8] In view of these multiple and contradictory definitions, theologians over the years have been like Lewis Carroll's Humpty Dumpty who said, "When I use a word it means just what I choose it to mean — neither more nor less." And George Wesley Buchanan was right when he asserted that interpreters have "internalized, de-temporalized, cosmologized, spiritualized, allegorized, mysticized, psychologized, philosophized, and socialized the concept of the Kingdom of God," attempting to make it workable for Christian thought.[9] This is not surprising. Should not the major subject Jesus spoke about two thousand years ago be at the heart of the Christian message today? For it not to be would be awkward.

In 1892, however, life-of-Jesus research was thrown into a tailspin with the publication in Germany of Johannes Weiss's book, *Jesus' Proclamation of the Kingdom of God.*[10] A mere sixty-seven pages in length, this book is possibly the most important work ever written in modern life-of-Jesus research. Prior to Weiss, theologians had sought valiantly to make the kingdom of God a pivotal concept for Christian theology. Weiss, more interested in historical research than in theological relevance, was the first modern New Testament scholar to take seriously the understanding of the kingdom that dominated the opening centuries of the Christian movement. He contended that for Jesus the kingdom was an eschatological concept and should be interpreted against a background of first-century Jewish eschatological expectations. "Eschatology" is based on a Greek word meaning "last" or "final." Thus eschatology is a branch of religious thought that speculates about final events in world and human history. Among Jesus' contemporaries, we now know, were Jews who believed the historical process was reaching its denouement, climax, or final hour. Something dramatic and cataclysmic was about to take place: the God of Israel was on the verge of intervening in human affairs in order to abolish injustice and to make things right on this earth.

Scholars know about these "end-of-the-world" or "eschatological" hopes and expectations as a result of the recovery and systematic study of a body of "crisis" writings called "apocalyptic literature."[11] Some Jewish thinkers were convinced the only way the injustices of this world, flawed with evil, could be rectified would be by God himself intervening in human affairs. A supernatural deliverance was needed and hoped for. This way of reasoning, reflected in works like Daniel in the Old Testament and the Revelation, which now stands at the end of the New Testament, was possibly borrowed from Zoroastrianism, the indigenous religion of Persia (Iran). Johannes Weiss argued that Jesus shared these eschatological hopes and consequently proclaimed the imminent coming of God's kingdom, a golden age to be inaugurated by God for repentant Jews. This position is widely accepted in scholarly circles, justifying Rudolf Bultmann's observation of a half-century ago, "Today nobody doubts that Jesus' conception of the Kingdom of God is an eschatological one."[12]

However, this view, although accepted in scholarly circles, has never been accepted or taken seriously by orthodox Christianity. The reason for its non-acceptance is obvious: consistent eschatology bluntly holds that Jesus was mistaken in what he preached. The kingdom he fervently believed would immediately appear did not come (the church came instead). Viewing Jesus as a mistaken prophet, in error about his main message, runs contrary to the "perfect teacher" image of him promulgated by guardians of orthodoxy.

Nowhere, regretfully, among Jesus' sayings is there a definition of the kingdom of God.[13] Evidently the gospel writers assumed their readers knew what this phrase meant. Nor is there reason to believe they recorded every detail of Jesus' teachings. Indeed, the recorded sayings probably represent only a fragment of Jesus' instruction. We must remember that all of Jesus' words recorded in the Synoptic Gospels can be read in about an hour's time; all his words about the kingdom of God, or kingdom of heaven, can be read in less than a half hour's time. Thus questions arise in our minds for which we have no answers. Where did Jesus expect the kingdom to come? Did he expect it to come in Galilee? Or perhaps at Jerusalem? How did Jesus expect the kingdom to come? Did he expect it to come down out of heaven on clouds of glory? It's impossible to answer these questions. But we do have a number of Jesus' kingdom pronouncements, and these pronouncements can be categorized. When categorized, they enable us to profile in an incomplete and indistinct manner Jesus' conception of the kingdom as a blessed place. A number of them deal with eating bread and drinking wine, and the survey of Jesus' kingdom pronouncements that follows will begin with these bread-and-wine sayings. Parenthetically, nowhere among Jesus' kingdom sayings is the kingdom of God defined as an "inner" phenomenon like peace of mind or peace of soul or the rule of God in human hearts. Nor did Jesus define the kingdom as a social-reform movement to abolish societal ills like slavery and slums.

After surveying Jesus' sayings about the kingdom, we will then be able to discover or determine what interpretive theory best "explains" the observations Jesus made about the kingdom. How can his kingdom sayings be made to "make sense" to the modern mind?

The Kingdom as a Place of Eating and Drinking

Statements that affirm that people will sit at tables, eat, and drink wine point in the direction of the kingdom as a place. Consider, for example, the discussion of the narrow door in Luke.

> Strive to enter by the narrow door; for many, I tell you, will seek to enter and will not be able. When once the householder has risen up and shut the door, you will begin to stand outside and to knock at the door, saying, "Lord, open

to us." He will answer you, "I do not know where you come from." Then you will begin to say, "We ate and drank in your presence, and you taught in our streets." But he will say, "I tell you, I do not know where you come from; depart from me, all you workers of iniquity!" There you will weep and gnash your teeth, when you see Abraham and Isaac and Jacob and all the prophets in the *kingdom of God* and you yourselves thrust out. And men will come from east and west, and from north and south, *and sit at table in the kingdom of God.* (Luke 13:24–29)

Or consider the following sayings, two of which Jesus uttered in the context of the Last Supper.

I tell you many will come from east and west and *sit at table with Abraham, Isaac, and Jacob in the kingdom of heaven,* while the sons of the kingdom will be thrown into the outer darkness; there men will weep and gnash their teeth.

(Matt 8:11–12)

And he took a cup, and when he had given thanks he gave it to them, saying, "Drink of it, all of you; for this is my blood of the covenant, which is poured out for many for the forgiveness of sins. I tell you *I shall not drink again of this fruit of the vine until that day when I drink it new with you in my Father's kingdom.*" (Matt 26:27–29 || Mark 14:25)

And when the hour came, he sat at table, and the apostles with him. And he said to them, *"I have earnestly desired to eat this Passover with you before I suffer; for I tell you I shall not eat it until it is fulfilled in the kingdom of God."* (Luke 22:14–16)

When one of those who sat at table with him heard this, he said to him, *"Blessed is he who shall eat bread in the kingdom of God!"* (Luke 14:15)

You are those who have continued with me in my trials; as my Father appointed a kingdom for me, so do I appoint for

you that *you may eat and drink at my table in my kingdom,* and
sit on thrones judging the twelve tribes of Israel.

(Luke 22:28–30)

An examination of these passages reveals numerous concrete
features about the kingdom. The apostles will have the honor
of eating and drinking at table with Jesus. Many will come
from east and west and sit at table with Abraham, Isaac, and
Jacob. Jesus anticipated eating Passover and drinking wine in
the kingdom. There is no indication he disagreed with the man
who exclaimed, "Blessed is he who shall eat bread in the kingdom of God," for it was in the context of this exclamation that
Jesus delivered the well-known banquet parable (Luke 14:16–
24). Also, in Matthew's gospel Jesus compared the kingdom to
a marriage feast (Matt 22:1–14). These multiple references to
eating bread, drinking wine, observing Passover, and sitting at
table with Abraham, Isaac, and Jacob show that for Jesus the
kingdom was a physical realm.

The Kingdom as a Place with Stations of Honor

Further evidence that Jesus thought of the kingdom as a physical
realm is seen in the idea of different ranks or stations of honor
in the kingdom. Consider, for example, the winsome story of the
request made for the sons of Zebedee.

> Then the mother of the sons of Zebedee came up to him,
> with her sons, and kneeling before him she asked him for
> something. And he said to her, "What do you want?" She
> said to him, "Command that these two sons of mine may
> sit, one at your right and one at your left, *in your kingdom.*"
> But Jesus answered, "You do not know what you are asking.
> Are you able to drink the cup that I am to drink?" They said
> to him, "We are able." He said to them, "You will drink my
> cup, but to sit at my right hand and at my left is not mine
> to grant, but it is for those for whom it has been prepared
> by my Father." (Matt 20:20–23)

That different ranks of honor will exist in the kingdom is suggested by the following passages:

> Whoever then relaxes one of the least of these command- ments and teaches men so, *shall be called least in the kingdom of heaven;* but he who does them and teaches them *shall be called great in the kingdom of heaven.* For I tell you, unless your righteousness exceeds that of the scribes and Pharisees, you will never enter the kingdom of heaven. (Matt 5:19–20)

> Truly, I say to you, among those born of women there has risen no one greater than John the Baptist; *yet he who is least in the kingdom of heaven* is greater than he. (Matt 11:11 || Luke 7:28)

> At that time the disciples came to Jesus, saying, "Who is the greatest in the kingdom of heaven?" And calling to him a child, he put him in the midst of them, and said, "Truly, I say to you, unless you turn and become like children, you will never enter the kingdom of heaven. Whoever hum- bles himself like this child, *he is the greatest in the kingdom of heaven."* (Matt 18:1–4)

In regard to status, Jesus believed that when the kingdom arrived his twelve primary disciples would rule the reconstituted or regathered tribes of Israel.

> As my Father appointed a kingdom for me, so do I appoint for you that you may eat and drink at my table in my king- dom, and sit on thrones judging the twelve tribes of Israel.
> (Luke 22:29–30)

> Truly I say to you, in the new world, when the Son of Man shall sit on his glorious throne, you who have followed me will also sit on twelve thrones, judging the twelve tribes of Israel. (Matt 19:28)

The strategic role the Twelve were to play in the soon-to-arrive kingdom is the reason for their refusal to leave Jerusalem after

Stephen's persecution. It was obligatory for them to remain in Jerusalem in order to assume the roles of tribal judges when the kingdom arrived.

Related to different ranks or stations is the belief that scribes and eunuchs will be in the kingdom.

> And he said to them, "Therefore every scribe who has been trained for the kingdom of heaven is like a householder who brings out of his treasure what is new and what is old." (Matt 13:52)

> For there are eunuchs who have been so from birth, and there are eunuchs who have been made eunuchs by men, and there are eunuchs who have made themselves eunuchs for the sake of the kingdom of heaven. He who is able to receive this, let him receive it. (Matt 19:12)

The Kingdom as a Place to Be Entered Bodily and to Be Seen with the Eye

Because the kingdom is a place, it will be possible for a person to enter it physically as though entering into a city or a house. When speaking of entering into a city or house, the New Testament writers commonly use the Greek verb *eiserchomai,* "to enter." They use this same verb when speaking of a person entering into the kingdom. Consider the following *eiserchomai* entry sayings.

> And if your eye causes you to sin, pluck it out; it is better for you to enter the kingdom of God with one eye than with two eyes to be thrown into hell.[14] (Mark 9:47)

> And Jesus looked around and said to his disciples, "How hard it will be for those who have riches to enter the kingdom of God!" (Mark 10:23 || Luke 18:24–25)

> For I tell you, unless your righteousness exceeds that of the scribes and Pharisees, you will never enter the kingdom of heaven. (Matt 5:20)

Other references to entering the kingdom appear in Matt 7:21;
18:3; 19:23–24; 23:13; Mark 10:15, 23, 24, 25; and Luke 18:17.
All these references indicate that for Jesus the kingdom was not
an abstract sovereignty; rather, it was a place or a land in which
people walk, sit, eat, and drink. It was possible to be thrown out
of the kingdom, and Jesus anticipated the physical removal of
the unrighteous.

> There you will weep and gnash your teeth, when you see
> Abraham and Isaac and Jacob and all the prophets in the
> kingdom of God and you yourselves thrust out.
>
> (Luke 13:28)

> I tell you, many will come from east and west and sit at
> table with Abraham, Isaac and Jacob in the kingdom of
> heaven, while the sons of the kingdom will be thrown into
> the outer darkness.[15] (Matt 8:11–12)

The idea of being thrown out of the kingdom is also found in
Matt 13:47–50.

The hypothesis that for Jesus the kingdom will be a realm or
land explains why the kingdom, on its arrival, will be visible to
the eye.

> Truly, I say to you, there are some standing here who will
> not taste death before they see the kingdom of God come
> with power. (Mark 9:1)

> Truly I say to you, there are some standing here who will
> not taste death before they see the Son of Man coming in
> his kingdom.[16] (Matt 16:28 || Luke 9:27)

> There you will weep and gnash your teeth, when you see
> Abraham and Isaac and Jacob and all the prophets in the
> kingdom of God and you yourselves thrust out.
>
> (Luke 13:28)

The Kingdom and the Satisfaction
of Material Needs

Pertinent to a discussion of the kingdom as a physical realm is a
passage from the Sermon on the Mount that teaches that those
who live in the kingdom will have their material needs satisfied.

> Therefore do not be anxious, saying, "What shall we eat?"
> or "What shall we drink?" or "What shall we wear?" For
> the Gentiles seek all these things; and your heavenly Father
> knows that you need them all. *But seek first his kingdom and
> his righteousness, and all these things shall be yours as well.*
> (Matt 6:31–33; italics added ‖ Luke 12:31)

The idea that in the kingdom the need for food will be satisfied
is repeated in the Lukan Beatitudes.

> And he lifted up his eyes on his disciples, and said: *"Blessed
> are you poor, for yours is the kingdom of God.* Blessed are you
> that hunger now, for you shall be satisfied. Blessed are you
> that weep now, for you shall laugh. Blessed are you when
> men hate you, and when they exclude you and revile you,
> and cast out your name as evil, on account of the Son of
> Man! Rejoice in that day, and leap for joy, for behold, your
> reward is great in heaven; for so their fathers did to the
> prophets." (Luke 6:20–23; italics added)

Because his followers would soon no longer concern themselves with food and clothing, Jesus exhorted them to live lives
of holy poverty.

> Fear not, little flock, for it is your Father's good pleasure to
> give you the kingdom. Sell your possessions, and give alms;
> provide yourselves with purses that do not grow old, with
> a treasure in the heavens that does not fail, where no thief
> approaches and moth destroys. For where your treasure is,
> there will your heart be also.[17] (Luke 12:32–34)

Jesus as the Doorkeeper to the Kingdom

Another indication of the kingdom's spatial nature is the teaching that people will enter the kingdom through a narrow door. Jesus will be the doorkeeper and will determine who is permitted or denied entrance.

> Not every one who says to me, "Lord, Lord," shall enter the kingdom of heaven, but he who does the will of my Father who is in heaven. On that day many will say to me, "Lord, Lord, did we not prophesy in your name, and cast out demons in your name, and do many mighty works in your name?" And then will I declare to them, "I never knew you; depart from me, you evildoers." (Matt 7:21–23)

The conception of entry into the kingdom through a narrow door is also found in Luke 13:22–29.

> He went on his way through towns and villages, teaching, and journeying toward Jerusalem. And some one said to him, "Lord, will those who are saved be few?" And he said to them, "Strive to enter by the narrow door; for many, I tell you, will seek to enter and will not be able. When once the householder has risen up and shut the door, you will begin to stand outside and to knock at the door saying, 'Lord, open to us.' He will answer you, 'I do not know where you come from.' Then you will begin to say, 'We ate and drank in your presence, and you taught in our streets.' But he will say, 'I tell you, I do not know where you come from; depart from me, all you workers of iniquity!' There you will weep and gnash your teeth, when you see Abraham and Isaac and Jacob and all the prophets in the kingdom of God and you yourselves thrust out. And men will come from east and west, and from north and south, and sit at table in the kingdom of God." (Luke 13:22–29)

A similar idea is suggested in the conclusion to the parable of the wise and foolish maidens.

Then the kingdom of heaven shall be compared to ten maidens who took their lamps and went to meet the bridegroom. Five of them were foolish and five were wise. For when the foolish took their lamps, they took no oil with them; but the wise took flasks of oil with their lamps. As the bridegroom was delayed, they all slumbered and slept. But at midnight there was a cry, "Behold, the bridegroom! Come out to meet him." Then all those maidens rose and trimmed their lamps. And the foolish said to the wise, "Give us some of your oil, for our lamps are going out." But the wise replied, "Perhaps there will not be enough for us and for you; go rather to the dealers and buy for yourselves." And while they went to buy, the bridegroom came, and those who were ready went in with him to the marriage feast; and the door was shut. Afterward the other maidens came also, saying, "Lord, Lord, open to us." But he replied, "Truly, I say to you, I do not know you." (Matt 25:1–12)

The image of the kingdom having a door is in the background of Matt 16:19, which states that the kingdom's keys will be entrusted to Peter. For Jesus the kingdom was like a city or fortress with a door or gate that will be locked, opened, and closed.

The Kingdom as the Antithesis of a Place of Torment

Repeatedly in Jesus' teachings the kingdom is juxtaposed with a place of torment. Jesus' contemporaries faced the alternatives of enjoying bliss in the kingdom or of enduring agony (frequently described as "weeping and gnashing of teeth") in a place of torment. Thus Mark 9:47–48 juxtaposes the kingdom of God and hell.

If your eye causes you to sin, pluck it out; it is better for you to enter the kingdom of God with one eye than with two eyes to be thrown into hell where their worm does not die, and the fire is not quenched.

Jesus' belief in a dual destiny is reflected in the Matthean interpretations (Matt 13:36–43, 47–50) given to the parables of the weeds and the fish net (both explicit kingdom parables):

> His disciples came to him saying, "Explain to us the parable of the weeds of the field." He answered, "He who sows the good seed is the Son of Man; the field is the world, and the good seed means the sons of the kingdom, the weeds are the sons of the evil one, and the enemy who sowed them is the devil; the harvest is the close of the age, and the reapers are angels. Just as the weeds are gathered and burned with fire, so will it be at the close of the age. The Son of Man will send his angels, and they will gather out of his kingdom all causes of sin and all evil doers, and throw them into the furnace of fire; there men will weep and gnash their teeth. Then the righteous will shine like the sun in the kingdom of their Father." (Matt 13:36b–43a)

> Again, the kingdom of heaven is like a net which was thrown into the sea and gathered fish of every kind; when it was full, men drew it ashore and sat down and sorted the good into vessels but threw away the bad. So it will be at the close of the age. The angels will come out and separate the evil from the righteous, and throw them into the furnace of fire; there men will weep and gnash their teeth.
>
> (Matt 13:47–50)

The weeping and gnashing of teeth detail crops up in Jesus' instruction about the narrow door (Luke 13:22–28). It appears in Jesus' laudatory comment about the centurion (Matt 8:10–13), a comment that juxtaposes the kingdom with "outer darkness":

> Truly, I say to you, not even in Israel have I found such faith. I tell you, many will come from east and west and sit at table with Abraham, Isaac, and Jacob in the kingdom of heaven, while the sons of the kingdom will be thrown into the outer darkness; there men will weep and gnash their teeth. (Matt 8:10b–12)

The Kingdom's Arrival as Near in Time

For Jesus the kingdom was not a remote goal of history — a dream to be realized hundreds or thousands of years in the future. Instead, the kingdom was an impending wonder. The most forceful of Jesus' sayings emphasizing the kingdom's nearness in time is his assertion preserved in Mark 9:1 (paralleled in Matt 16:28 and Luke 9:27): "And he said to them, 'Truly, I say to you, there are some standing here who will not taste death before they see the kingdom of God come with power.'" Or consider the Matthean summary of Jesus' message (Matt 4:17): "From that time Jesus began to preach, saying, 'Repent, for the kingdom of Heaven is at hand.'" Or observe the instructions Jesus gave his disciples before sending them out on their preaching mission (Matt 10:5–8): "These twelve Jesus sent out with the following instructions: 'Do not take the road to Gentile lands, and do not enter any Samaritan town; but go rather to the lost sheep of the house of Israel. And as you go proclaim the message: The kingdom of Heaven is at hand.'" Jesus told his disciples during the Last Supper that it was the last Passover he would celebrate with them before the kingdom came. This implies that he expected the kingdom's arrival before the next Passover, when he would again drink wine with them (Luke 22:15–18, Matt 26:29). That these Jesus sayings were preserved and transmitted by the gospel writers is remarkable. By the time these gospels were written (roughly between 70 and 100 c.e.) the generation that witnessed Jesus' ministry had died ("tasted death"). Jesus had erroneously predicted the kingdom would arrive before their deaths (Mark 9:1). That the gospel writers preserved this saying, containing a Jesus prophecy that did not materialize, is evidence of their integrity and accuracy as transmitters of what Jesus told his fellow Jews.

Thus, by way of summary, Jesus' kingdom teachings involved the following factors:

- Jesus expected a reconstitution of the tribes of Israel. He told his twelve disciples they would sit on thrones and judge the reconstituted tribes. They would also have the honor of sitting at Jesus' banquet table.

- Jesus conceived of himself as God's future viceroy in the kingdom of heaven. On each side of his throne will be places of honor reserved for those for whom they have been prepared.

- Entry into the kingdom will be through a narrow door. Jesus will be the doorkeeper and the door keys will be entrusted to Peter.

- Jesus anticipated the presence of Abraham, Isaac, Jacob, and the prophets. All will reappear and enjoy a good life in the kingdom, participating in a messianic banquet in which many from east and west will also participate.

- Apostate Jews will be expelled from the kingdom. Those expelled will (from a place of torment outside) look into the kingdom and behold the joys of those eating with Abraham, Isaac, and Jacob. Reflecting upon their unfortunate lot, they will weep and gnash their teeth. In contrast to this woeful existence, the righteous will shine like the sun in the kingdom of their Father (Matt 13:43).

- Passover will be observed in the kingdom. This observance will involve eating bread and drinking wine.

- Physical necessities (food and clothing) will be provided. Those excluded from the kingdom, however, will live in hunger (Luke 6:25).

- In the kingdom will be children, eunuchs, scribes, tax collectors, harlots, and the poor (Matt 21:31).

- Within the kingdom will be varying stations of honor. Some persons will be called great. Others will be called least.

- The entry sayings reveal that the kingdom will be a territory that can be entered bodily. It will also be a place that can be seen with the eye.

- Jesus expected the kingdom to arrive in the near future —
  within the lifetime of his listeners. He sent out messengers
  to announce to Jews, but not to Gentiles, the kingdom's
  near arrival.

Speaking in spatial categories, Jesus proclaimed the kingdom's imminent coming for repentant Jews. The gospel writers
portray Jesus as a prophet who drove himself relentlessly while
proclaiming the good news of the kingdom and who appointed
apostles to go to all the villages and cities in Israel to announce
that the kingdom was near (Luke 9:2, Matt 10:5–8).

The majority of Jesus' kingdom statements reveal that Jesus
thought of the kingdom as a blessed realm ("a heavenly city")
that was soon to appear on earth. At this point I call the reader's
attention to Appendix A and Appendix B. Appendix A cites every
verse in the Synoptic Gospels that contains the word "kingdom"
while Appendix B contains quotations from early church fathers
dealing with the kingdom of God. These verses and patristic quotations reveal that in early Christian thought the kingdom was a
blessed place and a future hope.[18] This understanding dominated
Christian thought until the time of Augustine, a fifth-century
theologian who identified the kingdom with the church. Christianity began as an eschatological-apocalyptic movement but
was gradually transformed into a belief system. Doctrine and
ritual supplanted eschatological enthusiasm.

Evidence suggests Jesus also expected other dramatic events
to occur in the near future. The Jewish temple in Jerusalem was
to be destroyed. The sun would be darkened, the moon would
no longer give its light, and stars would fall from heaven. National strife, famines, wars, and earthquakes would take place.
Jesus also foretold that a mysterious Son of Man would descend
on clouds from heaven with power and glory. This Son of Man
would send out angels, to the sound of a heavenly trumpet, to
gather the "elect" from the four winds and from the ends of the
earth to the ends of heaven.[19] Evidently these dramatic events
would occur close to the kingdom's arrival.

Thus Jesus' sayings taken in their totality compel the conclusion that the kingdom was his way of referring to a utopian realm or golden age for repentant Jews. This conception of the kingdom as a theocratic territory was expressed years ago by Johannes Weiss as follows:

> The Kingdom of God as Jesus thought of it is never something subjective, inward, or spiritual, but is always the objective messianic Kingdom, which usually is pictured as a territory into which one enters, or as a land in which one has a share, or as a treasure which comes down from heaven.[20]

For Jesus the kingdom was not a remote goal of human history; rather, it was an impending miracle. This kingdom's arrival, we can infer, would ipso facto abolish Roman control over Palestine. Consequently, in Roman eyes Jesus appeared to be an insurrectionist, and all four gospels agree that Jesus was crucified by Pontius Pilate on the charge of being a Jewish pretender to a throne.

The strength of this eschatological understanding of the kingdom is that it correlates, or harmonizes, with Jesus' recorded kingdom sayings. This interpretation enables us to make sense out of Jesus' kingdom pronouncements. Yet Christian apologists do not relish this interpretation. Such is the case because an eschatological view of the kingdom opens a Pandora's box of problems.

One of these problems is theological in nature. Theology involves systematic reflection upon the church's teachings, and across the centuries Christian spokesmen have assumed: "What Jesus taught is what the church teaches. A continuity exists between Jesus' proclamation and the church's proclamation." Capitulating to this longing for continuity, desiring to contemporize Jesus, Christians understandably want to believe that Jesus' kingdom teachings are a vital part of the Christian faith. They have gladly accepted Augustine's view that the kingdom is the church, or Adolf von Harnack's view that the kingdom is God's rule in human hearts, or Walter Rauschenbush's view that the kingdom is the exercise of the moral life in society. But these views, enticing as they are, are impossible to reconcile with Jesus' recorded sayings about the kingdom — sayings having to do with a reconstitution of the twelve tribes, with Passover observance, and with eating bread and drinking wine while sitting at banquet tables with Abraham, Isaac, and Jacob. Jesus' recorded sayings bring into focus the "strangeness," the "Jewishness," the "ideological remoteness" of Jesus' kingdom beliefs.[21]

A second problem broached by an eschatological interpretation of the kingdom is christological in nature. Christians want to believe Jesus was infallible. Most Christians are like my daughter, an Atlanta attorney, who remarked to me, "I've always believed Jesus had a direct telephone line to heaven." Christians reason: "Jesus was the Son of God and thus spoke the truth and nothing but the truth." Yet devotees of the eschatological view suggest Jesus was a mistaken prophet. Jesus expected the kingdom's swift arrival, but this expected kingdom did not appear. The church, filled with Gentiles, appeared instead.

I encountered this conception of Jesus as a mistaken prophet for the first time when I was a graduate student in seminary. This understanding of Jesus as a mistaken prophet troubled me then (in the 1950s); it troubles me now. I cringe when I read the following words written by Michael Grant, an historian:

> Jesus not only believed that God had ordered him to launch his Kingdom on earth, but he also maintained that this process would be completed very soon indeed: that the Day of the Lord was imminent, when God's will would reign everywhere, and the world, in some never wholly defined transcendent fashion would become perfect. This proved entirely wrong. The fulfillment did not take place, and has still not taken place. So, the whole ministry of Jesus was founded on a mistake.[22]

I also cringe when I read these sentences by Hans Küng, the Tübingen theologian:

The question then becomes so much more urgent: is not this proclamation of the Kingdom of God in the last resort simply a form of late Jewish apocalyptic? Is not Jesus ultimately an apocalyptic fanatic? Was he not under an illusion? In a word, was he not mistaken? Strictly speaking, we need not have any dogmatic inhibitions about admitting this in certain circumstances. To err is human. And if Jesus of Nazareth was truly man, he could also err. Of course there are some theologians who are more afraid of error in this connection than they are of sin, death, and the devil.[23]

This observation by Professor Küng reflects a third problem raised by an eschatological interpretation of the kingdom — a professional problem. Frequently overlooked is the institutional context within which theologians and New Testament scholars work. Many teach in denominational colleges or in seminaries where the mere questioning of Jesus' infallibility would be professional suicide. On ecclesiastical payrolls, they are expected to make Jesus' teachings meaningful and relevant. To believe Jesus was in error about his major message, the kingdom of God, is for them a closed option. Likewise, parishioners expect their pastors to believe in an infallible Jesus. They want to be told he was perfect. Thus accepting the view that Jesus was in error about his major message is a closed option for the clergy also. Moreover, the clergy (members of the religious establishment that controls what Christians believe about Jesus) mistakenly operates on the premise that Jesus' major message was not the kingdom of God but was himself. The clergy teaches parishioners: "Jesus viewed himself as the essence or subject of his teachings." They do this by concentrating on the letters of Paul and on the Fourth Gospel (which contains such secondary Jesus statements as "I am the way, the truth, and the life") to the exclusion of the Synoptic Gospels.

Christians, however, should not allow the possibility of unwelcome theological conclusions to influence biblical studies and historical research. Evidence should be followed regardless of where it leads. Christians do not serve God through intellectual dishonesty or gerrymandering evidence (evidence can be gerrymandered merely by excluding data).

Having expressed these caveats, I conclude with a reluctant observation: Jesus' kingdom preaching was predicated on a mistake. His fervent belief that a magnificent kingdom, primarily for Jews, would appear on earth within his listeners' lifetime was an error, an illusion, an unfulfilled hope. Attention will now be given to Jesus' attitude toward Gentiles.

Notes

1. Students of the New Testament should be aware that the term "gospel" is used in two different ways. On the lips of Jesus the term referred to the imminent arrival of the kingdom of God. But in the epistolary materials the term is used to refer to Jesus. Thus Paul could begin his letter to the Romans with a reference to "the gospel concerning his Son...Jesus Christ our Lord" (Rom 1:3–4). In one case the term refers to a message; in the other case it refers to the messenger.

2. John Reumann, *Jesus in the Church's Gospels: Modern Scholarship and the Earliest Sources* (Philadelphia: Fortress Press, 1968), 142.

3. The view of the kingdom as a curative power operative in Jesus' life and career was advanced by C. H. Dodd in his book entitled *The Parables of the Kingdom* (London: James Nisbet & Company, 1935). Professor Dodd's book has been influential in New Testament studies. The position he advanced and defended is known as "realized eschatology." I have evaluated Professor Dodd's reasoning in my book *Rethinking Realized Eschatology* (Macon, Ga.: Mercer University Press, 1988).

4. A classic presentation of this view is Walter Rauschenbusch, *A Theology for the Social Gospel* (Nashville: Abingdon Press, 1917. This book abounds with observations such as "The Kingdom is a fellowship of righteousness" (p. 134) and "The Kingdom of God is humanity organized according to the will of God" (p. 142). Rauschenbusch does not cite a statement of Jesus to justify these interpretations. The reason for this lack is obvious: there are none.

5. See Adolf von Harnack, *What Is Christianity?* (New York: Harper & Row, 1956). On p. 56 of this book von Harnack asserted the kingdom of God "is the rule of the Holy God in the hearts of individuals." The view that the kingdom is an inner possession of believers is a commonplace in liberal theology.

6. Kant quoted in John Macquarrie, *Jesus Christ in Modern Thought* (Philadelphia: Trinity Press International, 1990), 190.

7. Luke Timothy Johnson, *The Real Jesus* (San Francisco: HarperSanFrancisco, 1996), 38.

8. In Paragraph 567 on p. 145 of this catechism the text reads: "The King-dom of Heaven was inaugurated on earth by Christ.... The Church is the seed and beginning of this Kingdom." A similar view is expressed in Paragraph 541 on p. 138.

9. George Wesley Buchanan, *The Consequences of the Covenant* (Leiden: E. J. Brill, 1970), 55.

10. Johannes Weiss, *Jesus' Proclamation of the Kingdom of God* (trans. Richard Hyde Hiers and David Larrimore Holland; Philadelphia: Fortress Press, 1971). The German title of Johannes Weiss's book was *Die Predigt Jesu vom Reiche Gottes.*

11. The term "apocalyptic" is a play on the Greek word *apocalypsis,* which is the first word in the Revelation of St. John, the last book in the New Testa-ment. Apocalyptic literature is permeated with symbolism and with the belief that history is approaching its climax or end. The book of Daniel in the Old Tes-tament and the Revelation in the New Testament are examples of apocalyptic literature. Much Jewish apocalyptic literature was not included in either the Old or New Testaments. An excellent example of this noncanonical literature is 1 Enoch, quoted in the book of Jude in the New Testament (vv. 14–15). Nu-merous studies have been made of apocalyptic literature. A pioneering study is H. H. Rowley, *The Relevance of Apocalyptic* (New York: Association Press, 1964). Rowley's discussion includes the differences between prophetic and apocalyptic texts, synopses of apocalyptic books, and what he calls "the enduring message of apocalyptic." Note also Norman Cohn, *The Pursuit of the Millennium* (Fairlawn, N.J.: Essential Books, 1957); John Joseph Collins, *The Apocalyptic Imagination: An Introduction to the Jewish Matrix of Christianity* (New York: Crossroad Books, 1984); Christopher Rowland, *The Open Heaven: A Study of Apocalyptic in Judaism and Early Christianity* (New York: Crossroad Books, 1982). Recently published in three volumes is J. J. Collins et al., eds., *The Encyclopedia of Apocalypticism* (New York: Continuum Press, 1998).

12. Rudolf Bultmann, *Jesus Christ and Mythology* (New York: Charles Scrib-ner's Sons, 1958), 13.

13. Charles Guignebert, *Jesus* (trans. S. H. Hooke; New York: University Books, 1956), 330; Martin Dibelius, *Jesus* (trans. Charles B. Hendrick and Fred-erick C. Grant; Philadelphia: Westminster Press, 1939), 66: "Any attempt to interpret the individual sayings of Jesus about the Kingdom must be pre-ceded by a recognition of the fact that Jesus never specifically interpreted the expression 'Kingdom of God.'"

14. Notice that in this verse *basileia* or kingdom is paralleled with "hell."

15. With reference to the bodily expulsion of the unrighteous, observe the following quotation from the parable of the weeds: "The Son of Man will send his angels, and they will gather out of his kingdom all causes of sin and all evildoers, and throw them into the furnace of fire; there men will weep and gnash their teeth" (Matt 13:41–42).

16. In Matthean thought there is no sharp distinction between the kingdom of God and the kingdom of the Son of Man (cf. the parable of the weeds in Matt 13:24–30, 36–43).

17. The material blessings of the impending golden age are painted in glow-

ing terms in Matthew's Gospel: "And everyone who has left houses or brothers or sisters or father or mother or children or lands, for my name's sake, will receive a hundredfold and inherit eternal life" (Matt 19:29 || Luke 18:29–30).

18. Material in Appendix A and Appendix B has been appropriated from my book *Rethinking Realized Eschatology* (Macon, Ga.: Mercer University Press, 1988), 116–40.

19. Mark 13:2, 30; Mark 13:24–25; Matt 24:7; Mark 13:26; Mark 13:27.

20. Weiss, *Jesus' Proclamation,* 133.

21. One statement attributed to Jesus is used over and over by theologians who strive to make his kingdom teachings relevant for the Christian faith. That statement, found in Luke 17:21, asserts, "The kingdom of God is in the midst of you." Jesus directed this anomalous remark to the Pharisees. Moreover, the Pharisees had asked Jesus when the kingdom was coming, not where the kingdom was located (Luke 17:20–21). This passage, as many passages in the Bible, is difficult to interpret, evidently suggesting the kingdom's arrival was to be sudden, without any warning signs. Be that as it may, this irregular remark ("The kingdom of God is within you") is contrary to multiple remarks Jesus made indicating that for him the kingdom was a utopian place. Thus this unique remark, liberal theology's little red wagon, should not be the cornerstone assertion for determining Jesus' conception of the kingdom of God. Luke 17:21 is analyzed in detail in Appendix C.

22. Michael Grant, *Jesus: An Historian's Review of the Gospels* (New York: Charles Scribner's Sons, 1973), 193–94.

23. Hans Küng, *On Being a Christian* (New York: Doubleday, 1976), 217–18.

Chapter 2

What Was Jesus' Attitude
toward Non-Jews?

Today the Christian religion is almost exclusively a Gentile movement; this feature broaches the question: what was Jesus' attitude toward Gentiles (non-Jews)? Popular Christianity loves to portray Jesus as a humanitarian who cared deeply for them. "After all is said and done, he loved everybody." Certainly during Jesus' earthly career multiple opportunities abounded for him to have contacts with Gentiles and to relate positively to them. He lived his life in Galilee, the northern part of Palestine. In Matt 4:15 this area is described as "Galilee of the Gentiles." A dominant geographical feature of this area is the Sea of Galilee. The largest city on this sea in the first century was Tiberias, a Gentile city located a stone's throw from Capernaum, the fishing village used by Jesus as his base of operations. To the north of Galilee were the Syro-Phoenician cities of Tyre and Sidon. To the east were the Gentile areas of Gaulanitis, Hippos, and Gadara. To the south of Galilee was the Hellenistic territory of Scythopolis, the only Decapolis city located west of the Jordan River. The Gospels report that Jesus went into the region of the Decapolis but not into the cities themselves. Once he went "to the region of Tyre and Sidon" — two Gentile cities on the Mediterranean coast — but again there is no evidence he went into these non-Jewish cities.

Although Jesus was surrounded by Gentiles, the Gospels record few instances of him having personal contact with them. The most prominent instance of Jesus personally encountering a Gentile is the episode of the Canaanite woman.

Jesus then left that place and withdrew to the region of
Tyre and Sidon. And a Canaanite woman from those parts
came crying out, "Sir! Have pity on me, Son of David; my
daughter is tormented by a devil." But he said not a word
in reply. His disciples came and urged him: "Send her away;
see how she comes shouting after us." Jesus replied, "I was
sent to the lost sheep of the house of Israel, and to them
alone." But the woman came and fell at his feet and cried,
"Help me, sir." To this Jesus replied, "It is not right to take
the children's bread and throw it to the dogs." "True sir,"
she answered, "and yet the dogs eat the scraps that fall from
their master's table." Hearing this Jesus replied, "Woman,
what faith you have! Be it as you wish!" And from that
moment her daughter was restored to health.

(Matt 15:21–28)

Neither Jesus nor his disciples treated this woman kindly. To
be candid, they treated her in a churlish manner. At first Jesus
gave her the cold shoulder. Crying, the woman said, "Sir! Have
pity on me, Son of David; my daughter is tormented by a devil."
Jesus' cold response: He said not a word in reply. His disciples
joined the fray: "Send her away; see how she comes shouting
after us." Jesus then said to the woman, "I was sent to the lost
sheep of the house of Israel, and to them alone." The woman fell
at his feet and begged, "Help me, Sir." Exhibiting xenophobia,
Jesus remarked, "It is not right to take the children's bread and
throw it to the dogs." In an obsequious manner, the Canaanite
woman pled, "True, sir, and yet the dogs eat the scraps that fall
from their master's table." This dialogue between Jesus and the
Canaanite woman is neither amusing nor clever. Jesus insulted
the woman when he categorized her with dogs. That this ca-
nine remark was an insult eludes westerners who view dogs as
loveable household pets. In Jewish thought, however, the dog is
a scavenger (Exod 22:31) that eats its own vomit (Prov 26:11,
2 Pet 2:22). Paul classified dogs with evil workers (Phil 3:2) and
the Revelation of St. John, the last book in the New Testament,

asserts dogs will be excluded from heaven along with sorcerers, fornicators, murderers, idolaters, and those who love and practice falsehood (Rev 22:15). Jesus' classification of the Canaanite woman with a dog was for her a verbal kick in the face.

Jesus' view of Gentiles as dogs is probably the stimulus for his advice, "Do not give dogs what is holy; and do not throw your pearls before swine" (Matt 7:6). The categorizing of dogs and swine is found also in the quip of Rabbi Eleazar: "He who rears dogs is like one who rears swine." This same categorization is found in 2 Pet 2:22.

The fact is, Jesus had a condescending if not hostile attitude toward Gentiles. This derogatory attitude explains why he instructed his disciples "in praying do not heap up empty phrases as the Gentiles do; for they think they will be heard for their many words. Do not be like them" (Matt 6:7–8a). Jesus advised his hearers, "Do not be anxious, saying 'What will we eat?' or 'What shall we drink?' or 'What shall we wear?' For the Gentiles seek all these things" (Matt 6:31–32a). He categorized Gentiles with unpopular tax collectors. "For if you love those who love you, what reward have you? Do not even the tax collectors do the same? And if you salute only your brethren, what more are you doing than others? Do not even the Gentiles do the same" (Matthew 5:46–47). While giving counsel on how to react to a recalcitrant brother, Jesus advised, "let him be to you as a Gentile and tax collector" (Matt 18:17). In other words, Jesus used "Gentile" as a term of opprobrium.

Jesus sent out disciples to proclaim the imminent coming of the kingdom of God. In doing so he forbade them having any contact with Gentiles. Jesus instructed them, "Go nowhere among the Gentiles, and enter no town of the Samaritans, but go rather to the lost sheep of the house of Israel" (Matt 10:5–6). These instructions are reminiscent of Jesus' remark to the Canaanite woman, "I was sent to the lost sheep of the house of Israel, and to them alone."

Thus, contemporary efforts to present Jesus as a reformer in race relations or as a first-century civil rights worker are futile.

Proper race relations was not a concern to Jesus, who believed the trumpet had sounded and that the present world order was about to be turned upside down by the near arrival of God's kingdom.

Students of Jesus' thought must remember that the early church eventually confronted the issue of whether Gentiles could be disciples of Jesus. This matter appears prominently in Acts, our earliest church history, and also in the letters of Paul. This controversy over Gentile acceptance as Jesus' disciples would never have arisen in the primitive church had Jesus displayed an interest in Gentiles during his public ministry. Acts 10 reveals how controversial the issue of Gentile discipleship was. The major personalities in this controversy were Peter, the primary apostle, and Cornelius, a Gentile who was a centurion in the Roman army. Only after a puzzling "vision" of clean and unclean animals at Joppa was Peter willing to visit Cornelius at Caesarea. Peter was reflecting the mind of Jesus when he remarked to Cornelius and his Gentile friends, "You yourselves know how unlawful it is for a Jew to associate with or to visit any one of another nation" (Acts 10:28a). Moreover, students of early Christian origins who want to believe Jesus was interested in "converting" Gentiles must remember that he believed a Gentile proselyte, after converting to Judaism, was "twice as much a child of hell" as a scribe or Pharisee (Matt 23:15).

Our conclusion: The historical Jesus, capitulating to racial preference or prejudice, had a negative attitude toward Gentiles. He believed his mission was exclusively to Jews. Paul had a similar view when he wrote to the Galatians, "God sent forth his son, born of a woman, born under the law, to redeem those who were under the law" (Gal 4:4) and when he wrote to the Roman Christians, "For I tell you that Christ became a servant to the circumcised to show God's truthfulness, in order to confirm the promises given to the patriarchs" (Rom 15:8). The idea of Jewish exclusivity appears in Peter's observation made at Caesarea in the home of Cornelius: "Truly I perceive that God shows no partiality, but in every nation any one who fears him and does what is right is acceptable to him. You know the word which he sent to Israel, preaching good news of peace by Jesus Christ" (Acts 10:34–35). The historical Jesus made no effort to win Gentiles, whom he contemptuously referred to as dogs and pigs and whom he believed were responsible for his crucifixion (Matt 20:19).[1]

Notes

1. That Jesus viewed Gentiles as playing a crucial role in his crucifixion is reflected in these words (Matt 20:17–19): "And as Jesus was going up to Jerusalem, he took the twelve disciples aside, and on the way he said to them, 'Behold, we are going up to Jerusalem; and the Son of Man will be delivered to the chief priests and scribes, and they will condemn him to death, and deliver him to the Gentiles to be mocked and scourged and crucified, and he will be raised on the third day.' " These words, admittedly, may not be the *ipsissima verba* (the very words) of Jesus but instead may embody the thinking of the early church.

Chapter 3

What Were the Circumstances Surrounding Jesus' Birth?

So far we have given attention to two matters. What was Jesus' major message? And what was his attitude toward Gentiles? I propose we now give attention to circumstances that surrounded Jesus' birth.

Two of the four gospels in the New Testament contain accounts of Jesus' birth. These accounts, one in Matt 1–2 and the other in Luke 1–2, are commonly referred to as the "infancy narratives." In Matthew's account Joseph is the dominant character whereas in Luke's account Mary is the dominant character. In Matthew's narrative divine messages are conveyed through dreams while in Luke's narrative divine messages are conveyed by angels who physically appear to people like Mary and Elizabeth, mother of John the Baptist. In Matthew's version Mary and Joseph lived in Bethlehem; in Luke's version they lived in Nazareth. In Matthew's gospel Jesus' birth is celebrated by wise men who brought to the infant gifts of gold, frankincense, and myrrh; in Luke's gospel Jesus' birth is celebrated by shepherds and by a host of heavenly angels. In Luke's infancy account extensive attention is given to the birth of John the Baptist; Matthew's account lacks this emphasis. Matthew's version has the detail of the mysterious, guiding star and the account of the flight into Egypt to escape King Herod's threat of infanticide; Luke's version knows nothing of the star or the Herodian infanticide threat.

Both infancy narratives, however, have patrilineal genealogies and both contend Jesus was born of a virgin mother. I want us now to give attention to these two common (yet contradictory) features.

First of all, the genealogies reflect the view that a man named Joseph was Jesus' biological father. Across the years the church has never emphasized this idea. Rather, the church has always emphasized the belief that Jesus was a virgin's son. Yet embedded in the Gospels and in early Christianity is the opposite and contradicting tradition that Joseph, about whom little is known, was Jesus' biological father. In Matthew's gospel Jesus is called the carpenter's son (Matt 13:55). In the story about the youthful Jesus' Passover visit at age twelve to Jerusalem, Mary and Joseph are designated as Jesus' parents (Luke 2:41), and Mary referred to Joseph as Jesus' father (Luke 2:48). In John's gospel Jesus is referred to as Joseph's son (John 1:45): "Philip went to find Nathaniel, and told him, 'We have met the man spoken of by Moses in the Law, and by the prophets: it is Jesus son of Joseph, from Nazareth.'" In keeping with this father tradition, the Gospels of Matthew and Luke contain patrilineal genealogies tracing Jesus' ancestry back through Joseph. The inclusion of these patrilineal genealogies in the infancy narratives would be pointless apart from the view that Jesus was biologically Joseph's son. Admittedly these genealogies are confusing. Matthew's genealogy carries Jesus' ancestry back to Abraham (Matt 1:1–16) while Luke's longer genealogy carries Jesus' ancestry all the way back to Adam (Luke 3:23–38).

These lists, however, do not agree with one another. Matthew's genealogy from David to Joseph contains approximately twenty-seven names while Luke's genealogy from David to Joseph contains approximately forty-two names. Moreover, only four names (David, Shealtiel, Zerubbabel, and Joseph) in the David to Joseph lists are identical. The genealogies even give different names for Jesus' grandfather. In Matthew Jesus' grandfather is named Jacob; in Luke Jesus' grandfather is named Heli. Thus these two genealogies are contradictory.[1]

At the close of his patrilineal list Matthew attaches the idea that Jesus' genealogy consists of three times fourteen generations (Matt 1:17). This is a play on numerology. Written in Hebrew the name "David" is spelled with two different Hebrew letters. One is the Hebrew letter *daleth*. The other is the Hebrew letter *waw*. A *daleth* is the Hebrew symbol for the number four while the *waw* is the Hebrew symbol for the number six. In Hebrew the name "David" is spelled with two *daleths* (which together have a numerical value of eight) and one *waw* (with a numerical value of six). Eight plus six equals fourteen: the numerical value of "David" when the name is written in Hebrew. Matthew, employing numerology, was expressing the early Christian view that Jesus was the son of David. Thus he wrote:

> So all the generations from Abraham to David were fourteen generations, and from David to the deportation to Babylon fourteen generations, and from the deportation to the Christ fourteen generations. (Matt 1:17)

Matthew's genealogy has a puzzling feature. Four women, besides Mary, are mentioned: Tamar (1:3), Rahab (1:5), Ruth (1:5), and Bathsheba (1:6), who is not explicitly named but is referred to as "the wife of Uriah." All four of these women have flaws. Tamar committed incest when she seduced Judah, her father-in-law. Rahab was a pagan prostitute. Ruth was a foreigner from Moab. Bathsheba committed adultery with King David. Why does Matthew go out of his way to insert four flawed women in Jesus' ancestry? We don't know the answer to this question. But the mentioning of these four flawed women broaches possibilities Christian apologists don't belabor. Was Mary, Jesus' mother, somehow a flawed woman? Was Jesus' birth irregular? Was he born out of wedlock? Was Mary a prostitute? These questions can be pondered. Their answers are elusive. Be that as it may, both genealogies, in all probability, are pious fabrications by the apostolic church which, in the eyes of the church, provided Jesus with proper David credentials. These genealogies embody the view that Joseph was Jesus' biological father. Indeed, Matthew and Luke went out of their way to demonstrate through their genealogies that Jesus was descended through a Jew named

Joseph. These two genealogies would be meaningless and irrelevant if Joseph was not in fact Jesus' biological father. That Jesus was Joseph's biological son was a view held by an early Christian sect known as the Ebionites (a term meaning "the poor"). The Ebionites were "conservative" Jewish Christians. Tradition has it that this sect lasted well into the second century. Their first leader was James, Jesus' brother, and they continued choosing their bishops from Jesus' family. Accepting Jesus as the Messiah, they thought of themselves primarily as Jews. They rejected the belief that Jesus' death was a sin sacrifice. They interpreted the Lord's Supper as a memorial meal. But the most high-profile difference between the Ebionites and orthodox Christians was their rejection of the virgin birth.[2]

Toward the beginning of the second century, however, Jewish or Ebionite Christianity withered and was supplanted by Gentile Christianity. With this supplantation the Jewish understanding of Jesus as Joseph's biological son went into eclipse and was superceded by the contradictory virgin birth belief. I use the term "contradictory" because Jesus could not have been both a virgin's son with no human father, and biologically Joseph's son, having a human father. Belief in the virgin birth has dominated Christian thought for eighteen centuries. Sunday by Sunday millions of Christians gather in churches and confess in unison the Apostles' Creed, which asserts:

> I believe in God the father almighty and in Jesus Christ, his only son our Lord who was conceived by the Holy Spirit and born of the Virgin Mary.

The phrase "virgin birth," on reflection, is a misnomer. A more accurate phrase is "virginal conception." Virginal conception is not a Jewish idea. Indeed, *The Universal Jewish Encyclopedia* asserts "there is nothing in Jewish theology corresponding to this idea."[3] "The idea of a divine parenthood of human heroes was unknown in Judaism."[4] Nor is virginal conception a distinctly Christian belief. The post-Enlightenment discipline of comparative religion has made us aware that virginal conception was a widely-held belief in the pagan world of two millennia ago. For example, Hercules, Asclepius, Alexander the Great, and various Roman emperors were believed to be of divine parentage. The tradition existed that Plato experienced a virginal conception. Amphictione, Plato's mother, was impregnated by Apollo, the Greek and Roman god of sunlight, prophecy, music, and poetry. Ariston, Amphictione's husband, did not have sexual intercourse with her until after Plato's birth.[5] The virginal conception motif is found in Hinduism, Buddhism, and Zoroastrianism. Consider, for example, circumstances surrounding the birth of Siddhartha Gautama, Buddhism's founder. Tradition contends that Mahamaya, Siddhartha's mother, was taken to the Himalayas. There Siddhartha, the future Buddha, came to his mother in the form of a white elephant and entered her body through her right side. After his birth (which involved an exit through Mahamaya's right side) he took several steps, turned around and said, "This is my last time to be born."

The conclusion is obvious: virginal conception was a non-Jewish, pagan idea. The apostolic church, seeking to aggrandize Jesus, saw fit to apply this pagan belief to him. Both Matthew and Luke put forth the view that Jesus experienced a virginal conception. Matthew's gospel asserts this virginal conception was a fulfillment of a prophecy found in Isa 7:14. To understand Matthew's reasoning we must understand that Christian theology's earliest form was Old Testament proof texting. Christian thinkers ploughed the Old Testament for "proof texts" that could be viewed by Christians as "prophecies" of Jesus. They employed a Jewish interpretive technique known as *pesher*. *Pesher* is the Hebrew word for "interpretation." It appears in Eccl 8:1: "Who knows the interpretation of a thing." The *pesher* technique, used extensively in the Dead Sea Scrolls, involves taking an Old Testament statement out of its original context and giving to it a new interpretation or application. Matt 1:22–23 works a *pesher* on Isa 7:14. This Isaiah verse originally was a prophecy given in the eighth century before Christ to Ahaz, one of the kings of Judah. Ahaz feared an alliance that had been formed against him by Syria and Ephraim. Isaiah, desiring to encourage Ahaz, told him a "sign" would be given him by God. The text reporting this sign is found in Isa 7:14–16 and reads as follows:

> Therefore the Lord himself will give you a sign — Behold, a young woman (*almah*) shall conceive and bear a son, and shall call his name Immanuel. He shall eat curds and honey when he knows how to refuse the evil and choose the good. For before the child knows how to refuse the evil and choose the good, the land before whose two kings you are in dread will be deserted.

This prophecy of a young woman (*almah* in Hebrew) giving birth to a son referred originally to an event that was to occur during King Ahaz's reign, not to Jesus' birth several centuries later. Christian thinkers, attempting "to prove" Jesus' virginal conception, worked a *pesher* on this prophecy — applying it to Jesus. Their *pesher,* however, was not based on the Hebrew wording of Isa 7:14. Instead, their *pesher* was based on the Greek translation of Isa 7:14 that is found in the Septuagint, the Greek translation of the Old Testament produced some two or three centuries before Jesus lived. Unfortunately, the Septuagint mistranslated *almah* (the Hebrew word for "young woman") with the Greek word *parthenos,* which is the Greek word for "virgin." The Hebrew word for "virgin" is invariably *bethulah,* not *almah.* Thus the Old Testament basis used by the church "to prove" Jesus' virginal conception involves a mistranslation of the Hebrew noun *almah* in Isa 7:14. This verse, according to the Hebrew text, should begin: "Behold a young woman shall conceive...." It should not begin: "Behold a virgin shall conceive...." Nevertheless, this verse, taken out of context, mistranslated, and subjected to *pesher* exegesis, has played a primary role in establishing and maintaining the virgin birth belief in Christian theology.

In the New Testament the virgin birth is peripheral. The Gospels of Mark and John do not mention the belief. Nor does the Petrine literature, the book of Hebrews, or the Revelation of St. John. This belief does not appear at all in the apostolic preaching as reported in Acts. Paul never mentions this belief in his letters. To the contrary, he believed in the biological descent of Jesus from David. This is evident from his remark to the Roman Christians that Jesus came "from the seed of David according to the flesh" (Rom 1:3). The word used for "seed" in this statement is the Greek word "sperm." "Jesus came from the sperm of David."

Be that as it may, scores of Christians live under the illusion that the Christian religion "stands or falls" on the virgin birth of Jesus. This belief is one of the five basic beliefs of Protestant fundamentalism. It is also a cornerstone belief in Roman Catholic theology.

Was Jesus a virgin's son? The answer, I suggest, is *no*. The pagan virgin birth belief, historians now recognize, was one of the first steps taken by the early church in the simultaneous de-Judaizing of and hellenizing of the Christian message as it spread into the Greco-Roman world. Parenthetically, frequent reference is made in Christian discourse to the "miracle" of the virgin birth. But, on reflection, could a "virgin" birth be more miraculous (astonishing, mysterious) than a natural birth? I don't think so.

Notes

1. Matthew's genealogy (Matt 1:6–17): *David,* Solomon, Rehoboam, Abijah, Asa, Jehoshaphat, Joram, Uzziah, Jotham, Ahaz, Hezekiah, Manasseh, Amos, Josiah, Jechoniah, *Shealtiel, Zerubbabel,* Abiud, Eliakim, Azor, Zadok, Achim, Eliud, Eleazar, Matthan, Jacob, *Joseph.* Luke's genealogy (Luke 3:23–31): *David,* Nathan, Mattatha, Menna, Melea, Eliakim, Jonam, Joseph, Judah, Simeon, Levi, Matthat, Jorim, Eliezer, Joshua, Er, Elmadam, Cosam, Addi, Melchi, Neri, *Shealtiel, Zerubbabel,* Rhesa, Joanan, Joda, Josech, Semein, Mattathias, Maath, Naggai, Esli, Nahum, Amos, Mattathias, Joseph, Jannai, Melchi, Levi, Matthat, Heli, *Joseph.* The italicized names (*David, Shealtiel, Zerubbabel, Joseph*) are the only names in these two genealogies that are identical. Otherwise, the genealogies disagree with one another.

2. This rejection is dealt with by Irenaeus of Lyon, a church father who died ca. 202 c.e. and who wrote a work entitled *Against Heresies.* At one point in this work he asserts about the Ebionites, "Their interpretation is false, who dare to explain the Scripture thus: Behold, a girl (instead of a virgin) shall

conceive and bear a son. That is how the Ebionites say that Jesus is Joseph's natural son. In saying this they destroy God's tremendous plan for salvation" (III.21.1). At another point Irenaeus observes about the Ebionites, "The Ebionites are foolish.... For they refuse to realize that the Holy Spirit came over Mary, and the power of the Most High overshadowed her.... Thus they deny the heavenly wine and wish to know nought but the water of this world" (V.1.3). Similar remarks were made by Eusebius of Caesarea, a fourth-century church historian and contemporary of Constantine. Eusebius wrote a significant work entitled *Ecclesiastical History.* In this work he describes the Ebionites as folk who believed Jesus "had been born naturally from Mary and her husband" (III.27). At another place he observes, "Those who belong to the heresy of the Ebionites affirm that Christ was born of Joseph and Mary, and suppose him to be a mere man" (XI.17).

3. See p. 425 of the article on virgin births in Volume 10 of *The Universal Jewish Encyclopedia* (10 vols.; New York: Universal Jewish Encyclopedia Company, Inc., 1943), 10:425.

4. Ibid.

5. This tradition concerning Plato is found in Chapter 37 of Book I of Origen's *Against Celsus.* See A. Cleveland Coxe, ed. *Fathers of the Third Century* (vol. 4 of *The Ante-Nicene Fathers;* ed. Alexander Roberts and James Donaldson; Grand Rapids, Mich.: Eerdmans, 1956), 412.

Chapter 4

What Did Jesus Think about God?

Up to this point we have dealt with three questions. What was Jesus' major message? What did he think about Gentiles? What circumstances surrounded his birth? We come now to consider a fourth question: What did Jesus think about God? This question will strike some readers as a strange query. If any belief is widespread in orthodox Christianity, that belief is: Jesus was God and Jesus is God. "He is one of the blessed Trinity." Thus to inquire about what Jesus thought about God is — so some would argue — an absurd enterprise.

This belief, Jesus equals God, is hard to defend, however, when one gives attention to all the statements made by the historical Jesus that are relevant to this issue. The fact is, by no stretch of the imagination did Jesus elevate himself to the status of God. Instead, he viewed himself as a person living in relationship to God.

The distinction Jesus made between himself and God is evident in his response to an inquiry made to him one day about inheriting eternal life. This eternal-life inquiry appears in all three of the Synoptic Gospels. Mark's account reads as follows:

And as he was setting out on his journey, a man ran up and knelt before him, and asked him, "Good teacher, what must I do to inherit eternal life?" And Jesus said to him, "Why do you call me good? No one is good but God alone."

(Mark 10:17–18)

In this retort Jesus distinguished himself from God. To paraphrase Jesus' response: "The designation 'good' should not be applied to me but to God who alone is good. Don't call me good because I am not God."

A distinction between Jesus and God is implied in Jesus' prayer life. The Gospels report that Jesus on numerous occasions prayed. For example, "And in the morning, a great while before day, he rose and went out to a lonely place and there he prayed" (Mark 1:35). On one occasion he went into the hills and prayed all night (Luke 6:12). Jesus prayed in Gethsemane before his betrayal by Judas (Mark 14:35–36). His prayer life poses questions. Assuming Jesus was God, why did he pray to God? Does God pray to God? God praying to God is a puzzling idea. Contrarily, in his prayer life we sense Jesus' humanity — his identity with us. Unless we want to believe his prayer life was a ruse, it is impossible to accept the orthodox view that Jesus was none other than God himself (the Second Person of the Trinity) disguised in human form. Additionally, at no point, we must remember, did Jesus instruct his disciples to pray to him. Instead, he instructed them to pray to the heavenly Father who resides in the sky ("Our Father who art in heaven").

The distinction between God and Jesus becomes most obvious in his poignant cry of dereliction (Mark 15:34). While suffering crucifixion, Jesus cried with a loud voice, "My God, my God, why hast thou forsaken me?" Assuming Jesus was God, how can God abandon God? The answer is not obvious. By the fourth century the church had elevated Jesus to the status of God. But this elevation to divine status does not agree with Jesus' understanding of himself. Instances in the New Testament where Jesus is clearly referred to as God can be numbered on the fingers of one hand.

What did Jesus think about God? Like other first-century Jews, he believed God lived above this earth in the sky. This is not surprising. The sky, or heaven, was the home or mailing address of God in a prescientific age. Jesus taught his disciples to address God as "Father" and to pray, "Our Father who art in heaven" (i.e., "our Father-God who resides spatially up in the sky"). In heaven, Jesus believed, God's will is done (Matt 6:10). He taught that from heaven God observes "in secret" human behavior on this earth (Matt 6:4,6).

No trace of pantheism or panentheism is found in Jesus' teachings. Instead, Jesus had an anthropomorphic (human in shape) conception of God. He believed God sat on a throne located in the sky (Matt 5:34; 23:20–22). God has a face that is constantly contemplated by angels (Matt 18:10). He also has a finger (Luke 11:20) and hands (Luke 23:46). That the pure in heart shall someday "see God" implies God is visible (Matt 5:8). The long ending to Mark's gospel observes (Mark 16:19) that at the end of his life Jesus was "taken up into heaven and sat down at the right hand of God" (again implying God is visible, has hands, and sits on a throne like an oriental monarch).

Heaven, the abode of God and angels (Matt 22:30), was not far off. Instead, it was close to earth. Indeed, the Gospels presuppose a compact universe. At Jesus' birth a heavenly star, like a spotlight, led eastern wise men as they traveled six miles from Jerusalem to Bethlehem (Matt 2:9). At his baptism Jesus saw the heavens opened (Mark 1:10) and heard a voice from heaven speaking to him (Mark 1:11). On one occasion, Jesus believed, fire and brimstone rained down from heaven and destroyed the wicked city of Sodom (Luke 17:29). He believed that in the time of Elijah heaven was shut up for three years and six months (Luke 4:25).

Jesus conceived of God as being benevolent. He thought of God as one who makes his sun rise on the evil and the good (Matt 5:45), sends rain on the just and the unjust (Matt 5:45), feeds the birds of the air (Matt 6:26), clothes the grass of the field (Matt 6:30), and is kind to the ungrateful and selfish (Luke 6:35). He is merciful (Luke 6:36) and to this merciful God Jesus turned at the moment of his death: "Father, into thy hands I commit my spirit" (Luke 23:46).

I want us now to ponder a fifth question: What kind of ethical teacher was Jesus?

Chapter 5

What Kind of Ethical Teacher Was Jesus?

Back in 1896 Charles Sheldon, a clergyman in Topeka, Kansas, published a religious novel entitled *In His Steps*. This novel has sold millions of copies and has been translated into scores of languages. Today *In His Steps* is distributed for free by the Billy Graham evangelical organization. The book's first chapter begins with a quotation from 1 Pet 2:21, "For here unto were ye called; because Christ also suffered for you, leaving you an example, that ye should follow his steps." On the basis of this verse Sheldon's novel contends that Christians should "walk in the steps" of Jesus. When making an ethical decision they should ask: What would Jesus do if he were making this decision? The Reverend Henry Maxwell, the novel's main character and a pastor in Raymond, Kansas, asks himself: What would Jesus do if he (like me) were a pastor in Raymond, Kansas? The Reverend Maxwell answers this question among other things as follows: Jesus would preach against the saloon in Raymond, would identify with the great causes of humanity, would preach fearlessly against church hypocrites, and would give up a summer trip to Europe. Why Jesus would abandon a summer trip to Europe is not clear. What is clear is that the fictional Reverend Maxwell, like many Christian interpreters, conceived of Jesus as an ethicist who spoke out against society's evils, identified with great causes of humanity, and provided disciples with guidelines for personal behavior. In view of this widespread conception of Jesus as an ideal or model ethical teacher I propose we grapple with two questions. First of all, did Jesus speak out against society's evils and identify with

45

great causes of humanity? Secondly, did he provide his disciples with sensible guidelines for personal behavior?

The first of these questions must be answered with a no. Jesus had little, if anything, to say about society's problems. Nor did he identify with great causes of humanity, like pacifism and social justice.

Nowhere, for example, does Jesus condemn human slavery. Instead, taking slavery for granted, he used slaves as characters in his parables. Thus he spoke of a man going on a journey and entrusting his property to his slaves (Matt 25:14) and of a host sending out his slave to inform invited guests that a banquet was ready (Luke 14:17). Repeatedly in his parables Jesus used the common Greek word for slave (*doulos*). Modern translators soften this slave word by translating it with the less offensive word "servant." Throughout the New Testament slavery is viewed as an acceptable societal institution. Slavery was a part of the first century's cultural landscape. Thus before the Civil War the southern clergy, as their sermons reveal, defended slavery by appealing to Jesus' parables and by appealing to epistolary slave passages like Eph 6:5–9 wherein Paul advised slaves to be obedient to their masters.

Nowhere does Jesus condemn governmental brutality. The Roman Empire, personified in a feral Roman bureaucrat like Pontius Pilate, could be savage in dealing with Jews. Jesus was told about Galileans whose blood Pilate mingled with their sacrifices. He responded to this slaughter with the puzzling words, "Do you think these Galileans were worse sinners than all the other Galileans, because they suffered this? I tell you, No; but unless you repent you will all likewise perish" (Luke 13:2–3). Some three decades after Jesus' crucifixion the Jews (out of desperation) revolted against the Roman Empire. But Jesus' attitude toward Roman authority was, "Render to Caesar the things that are Caesar's" (Mark 12:17). His attitude on poverty was revealed in his casual yet realistic remark, "You have the poor with you always" (Matt 26:11).

Nor did Jesus condemn racial divisions and antagonisms. Displaying racial prejudice, he called Gentiles dogs and instructed his disciples to have nothing to do with them.

Jesus' lack of concern for societal problems like slavery is understandable. He believed history's grand finale was near. In the immediate future the kingdom of God would appear on earth and its arrival would ameliorate societal woes. The hungry would be satisfied and the sorrowful would laugh (Luke 6:20–21). This utopian world for Jews would be God's doing; it would not be brought about through human endeavor or social engineering.

Whereas he did not talk about societal issues, Jesus did on occasion provide moral guidelines dealing with personal conduct. These guidelines are concerned with one-on-one relationships. They were not given systematically but were given for specific problems or situations.

Moreover, Jesus' moral teachings on personal behavior are rooted in Judaism. Jesus does not portray himself as an original, creative ethicist, "thinking thoughts no one else has ever thought." Rather he spoke and thought as a Jew.

Probably the most familiar of Jesus' ethical norms is the Golden Rule found in the Sermon on the Mount: "Do unto others as you would have them do unto you; for this is the law and the prophets" (Matt 7:12). It should be noted that Jesus defined the Golden Rule as a summary of both the law, Torah, and the Jewish prophets. This definition shows he reasoned as a rabbi. On one occasion (Matt 22:34–40) he was asked by a Pharisee, "Teacher, which is the great commandment in the law?" Jesus did not say, "I'm so glad you asked that. I shall now be a creative ethicist and tell you a novel commandment no one has ever thought about." Instead, appealing to his Jewish heritage, reasoning as a rabbi, he quoted Deut 6:4 ("Hear, O Israel: the Lord our God is one Lord, and you shall love the Lord your God with all of your heart, and with all of your soul, and with all your might") and Lev 19:18b ("You shall love your neighbor as yourself"). Hovering in the background of the Pharisee's question ("Which is the great commandment in the law?") is the pious, third-century tradition in Judaism that in the law (Torah) are no less than

613 commandments. This legal tradition contends that 365 of the 613 commandments are negative ("do not do this") while 248 are positive ("do this"). Thus Jesus chose Deut 6:4 and Lev 19:18b as the two greatest commandments in the 613.

Jesus viewed proper moral behavior as the key to inheriting eternal life. When asked what one must do to have eternal life, Jesus answered, "If you would enter life, keep the commandments" (Matt 19:16–19). He then cited commandments dealing with killing, adultery, stealing, bearing false witness, honoring parents, and loving neighbors.

Some of Jesus' moral teachings strike contemporary readers as draconian. Consider Matt 5:29–30: "If your right eye causes you to sin, pluck it out and throw it away; it is better that you lose one of your members than that your whole body be thrown into hell. And if your right hand causes you to sin, cut if off and throw it away; it is better that you lose one of your members than that your whole body go into hell." Particularly severe are his teachings on sexuality and family relationships. While considering these familial pronouncements we must bear in mind that no evidence suggests Jesus, unlike Muhammad, married or fathered children. To our knowledge he never supported a family, cared for a sick son or daughter, or coped with a nagging wife. Having never experienced a loveless or frayed marriage and having never gone through the trials and tribulations of wedlock, Jesus soundly condemned divorce. His divorce condemnation has been transmitted in two severe versions. Mark 10:11–12 asserts, "Whoever divorces his wife and marries another, commits adultery against her; and if she divorces her husband and marries another, she commits adultery." Matthew 5:32, containing the unchastity exception, asserts, "Every one who divorces his wife, except on the ground of unchastity, makes her an adulteress; and whoever marries a divorced woman commits adultery." Thus Jesus viewed the remarriage of a divorced man or woman as adultery. Evidently Jesus' opinion was "once married, always married. If your marriage is an unhappy one, that's too bad for you."

Jesus' remarks about family relationships are also severe. Consider Luke 14:26, "If any one comes to me and does not hate his own father and mother and wife and children and brothers and sisters, yes, and even his own life, he cannot be my disciple." Or consider the variant found in Matt 10:37, "He who loves father or mother more than me is not worthy of me; and he who loves son or daughter more than me is not worthy of me." These statements veer toward megalomania.

At one point in Jesus' career his mother and brothers came to where he was and asked to speak with him. Being informed of their presence, Jesus remarked, "Who is my mother, and who are my brothers?" And stretching out his hand toward his disciples, he said, "Here are my mother and my brothers! For whoever does the will of my Father in heaven is my brother and sister and mother" (Matt 12:48–50). In this statement Jesus repudiated traditional family relationships. Indeed, Jesus encouraged the disruption of family relationships. On one occasion (Luke 12:49–53) he asserted: "I came to cast fire upon the earth; and would that it were already kindled! I have a baptism to be baptized with; and how I am constrained until it is accomplished! Do you think that I have come to give peace on earth? No, I tell you, but rather division; for henceforth in one house there will be five divided, three against two and two against three; they will be divided, father against son and son against father, mother against daughter and daughter against her mother, mother-in-law against her daughter-in-law and daughter-in-law against her mother-in-law."

Preachers preaching sermons on the family are hard pressed to find appropriate Jesus quotations to use as texts for their sermons. Likewise, while conducting wedding services, they are hard pressed to find appropriate Jesus quotations to use. The best they can do is allude to his singular visit to a wedding in Cana of Galilee (as recounted in John 2:1–11).

Why churches promulgate "Christian" weddings and a belief in "Christian" marriage is puzzling. Jesus was not married. He rejected the idea of marriage in a future life. This rejection came in the context of an attempt by Sadducees to befuddle Jesus on the issue of marriage.

> Next Sadducees came to him. (It is they who say that there is no resurrection.) Their question was this: "Master, Moses laid it down for us that if there are brothers, and one dies leaving a wife but no child, then the next should marry the widow and carry on his brother's family. Now there were seven brothers. The first took a wife and died without issue. Then the second married her, and he too died without issue. So did the third. Eventually the seven of them died, all without issue. Finally the woman died. At the resurrection, when they come back to life, whose wife will she be, since all seven had married her?" Jesus said to them, "You are mistaken, and surely this is the reason: you do not know either the scriptures or the power of God. When they rise from the dead, men and women do not marry; they are like the angels in heaven." (Mark 12:18–25)

Thus Jesus believed marriages would not exist in the future world because people would be like sexless angels. The linking of celibacy and eternal life is found also in the Jesus statement recorded in Luke 20:34–36: "The sons of this age marry and are given in marriage; but those who are accounted worthy to attain to that age and to the resurrection from the dead neither marry nor are given in marriage, for they cannot die any more, because they are equal to angels and are sons of God, being sons of the resurrection." Thus in Jesus' thought marriage was a feature of "this age," but those who aspire to the resurrection from the dead, an existence superior to "this age," would not marry.

Paul shared Jesus' point of view. His negative attitude toward sexuality and marriage is spelled out in his first letter to the Corinthian church.

> Now concerning the matters about which you wrote. It is well for a man not to touch a woman. But because of the temptation to immorality, each man should have his

own wife and each woman her own husband. The husband
should give to his wife her conjugal rights, and likewise
the wife to her husband. For the wife does not rule over
her own body, but the husband does; likewise the husband
does not rule over his own body, but the wife does. Do not
refuse one another except perhaps by agreement for a season, that you may devote yourselves to prayer; but then
come together again, lest Satan tempt you through lack of
self-control. I say this by way of concession, not of command. I wish that all were as I myself am. But each has
his own special gift from God, one of one kind and one of
another. To the unmarried and the widows I say that it is
well for them to remain single as I do. But if they cannot
exercise self-control, they should marry. For it is better to
marry than to be aflame with passion. (1 Cor 7:1–9)

This passage reveals that Paul believed never touching a
woman was a commendable practice ("It is well for a man not
to touch a woman"). He viewed marriage as a solution to an in-
tractable libido ("For it is better to marry than to be aflame with
passion"). And he applauded celibacy ("I wish that all were as
I myself am"). Paul went so far as to advise husbands to live as
though they had no wives (1 Cor 7:29). Despite all this negativity, the medieval church saw fit to view marriage as one of
the seven sacraments. They did so by appealing to the Latin
Vulgate's translation of Eph 5:23–33. In this Ephesian discussion of marriage and husband-wife relationships the following
statement appears in the Vulgate translation of 5:32: "This is a
great sacrament." On the basis of this Latin statement Thomas
Aquinas and other medieval thinkers elevated marriage to the
status of a sacrament, along with baptism and the Eucharist.
Unfortunately, the Latin word *sacramentum* in Eph 5:32 is a mistranslation of the Greek word *mysterion* ("mystery"). Thus the
verse should be translated, "This is a great mystery" rather than
"This is a great sacrament." Building beliefs on mistranslated
Greek words, as Thomas Aquinas did, is not the wisest of theo-

logical procedures. No biblical justification exists for viewing marriage as a sacrament.

Jesus viewed human sexuality with jaundiced eye. He viewed sexual attraction, the unsought arousal of the libido, as lust. "You have heard that it was said, 'You shall not commit adultery.' But I say to you that everyone who looks at a woman lustfully has already committed adultery with her in his heart" (Matt 5:28). Jesus approved of castration if performed for the kingdom of God (Matt 19:12).

The intensity or severity of Jesus' ethical pronouncements has led scholars like Albert Schweitzer to conclude that his ethical teachings should be understood as interim in nature, i.e., ethical teachings for the brief interval (interim) between Jesus' public ministry and the imminent arrival of the kingdom of God. Adherents to this interim theory reject the view that Jesus' moral teachings constitute a permanently valid ethical system intended for all times. Understandably, Christian apologists find this interim theory distasteful. They fear it undercuts Jesus' authority and relevance for contemporary moral life.

Be that as it may, the church over the centuries has adroitly gerrymandered Jesus' ethical pronouncements. Some they emphasize. Others they pass over. I know of no Christian who subscribes to the begging and borrowing behavior commended in Matt 5:42, "Give to him who *begs* from you, and do not refuse him who would *borrow* from you." This *borrowing* command, if followed pell-mell, would lure Christians into bankruptcy. And the *begging* command, if followed indiscriminately, would delight San Francisco panhandlers but would bring upon Christians all kinds of financial woes. Hence these borrowing and begging commands are ignored.

Also neglected by most disciples is Jesus' anti-wealth and pro-poverty admonition expressed in Matt 6:19, "Do not lay up for yourselves treasures on earth, where moth and rust consume and where thieves break in and steal." Yet few Christians take vows of poverty. They lay up for themselves treasures on earth. They wisely believe in saving for a rainy day. "If I don't take care of myself, who will?" They want to pass on assets to children and grandchildren. In this regard they differ from Jesus, who manifested a cavalier attitude toward wealth. He advised one listener (Matt 19:21) to sell all his possessions and give to the poor. On another occasion he refused to become involved in an inheritance dispute between siblings. Instead, he rebuked the complainant who had been defrauded by his brother, "Man, who made me a judge or divider over you?" (Luke 12:13–14). Since the kingdom was near, Jesus advised his disciples, "Sell your possessions and give alms; provide yourselves with purses that do not grow old, with a treasure in the heavens that does not fail, where no thief approaches and no moth destroys" (Luke 12:33).

Jesus was hostile toward wealthy people, a hostility that members of the clergy often downplay when appealing to the wealthy for ecclesiastical funds. He affirmed, "It is easier for a camel to go through the eye of a needle than for a rich man to enter the kingdom of God" (Mark 10:25). The classic example of Jesus' attitude toward persons of wealth is his parable about the rich man and Lazarus.

> There once was a rich man, who dressed in purple and the finest linen, and feasted in great magnificence every day. At his gate, covered with sores, lay a poor man named Lazarus, who would have been glad to satisfy his hunger with the scraps from the rich man's table. Even the dogs used to come and lick his sores. One day the poor man died and was carried away by the angels to be with Abraham. The rich man also died and was buried, and in Hades, where he was in torment, he looked up; and there, far away, was Abraham with Lazarus close beside him. "Abraham, my father," he called out, "take pity on me! Send Lazarus to dip the tip of his finger in water, to cool my tongue, for I am in agony in this fire." But Abraham said, "Remember, my child, that all the good things fell to you while you were alive, and all the bad to Lazarus; now he has his consolation here and it is you who are in agony. But that is not

all: there is a great chasm fixed between us; no one from our side who wants to reach you can cross it, and no one may pass from your side to us." "Then, father," he replied, "will you send him to my father's house, where I have five brothers, to warn them, so that they too may not come to the place of torment." But Abraham said, "They have Moses and the prophets; let them listen to them." "No, father Abraham," he replied, "but if someone from the dead visits them, they will repent." Abraham answered, "If they do not listen to Moses and the prophets they will pay no heed even if someone should rise from the dead."

(Luke 16:19–31)

This parable does not state that the rich man was an evil person and that Lazarus was a noble fellow. Yet both died. One went to hell; the other went to a place of bliss. The reason implied for their different destinies: one was rich while the other one was poor. This parable has a sadistic flavor. The rich man is tormented in hell with flames of fire. His request for water is denied. His request for a warning to be given to his five brothers is also rejected. And Abraham taunts him, "Son, remember that you in your lifetime received your good things, and Lazarus in like manner evil things; but now he is comforted here, and you are in anguish." This taunt suggests Jesus' woe of Luke 6:24, "Woe to you that are rich, for you have received your consolation." This hostility toward wealthy people probably was engendered by Jesus' peasant or proletarian upbringing. His wealth denunciations go a long way toward explaining why some people view Christianity as a poor man's religion. Moreover, Jesus' belief, and the church's belief, in a hell where the damned will be eternally tormented prompted Charles Darwin, father of the evolution theory, to observe he could not understand why any person would want the Christian faith to be true. Darwin wrote, "I can indeed hardly see how anyone ought to wish Christianity to be true; for if so the plain language of the text seems to show that the men who do not believe, and this would include my Father, Brother and almost all my best friends, will be everlastingly punished. And this is a damnable doctrine."[1]

Jesus, eschatological prophet who believed he was God's trumpet to proclaim to Jews the good news of the kingdom's near arrival, was on occasion an ethical teacher. His specific moral teachings were personal, not social. He made no attempt "to reform" pagan society. Some of his ethical rules are impractical and are understandably ignored by Christians. Particularly pusillanimous is his advice, "If any one strikes you on the right cheek, turn to him the other also; and if any one would sue you and take your coat, let him have your cloak as well; and if any one forces you to go one mile, go with him two miles" (Matt 5:39–41).

> To put the matter now most sharply, Jesus does not provide a valid ethics for today. His ethical teaching is interwoven with his imminent eschatology to such a degree that every attempt to separate the two and to draw out only the ethical thread invariably and inevitably draws out also strands of the eschatology, so that both yarns only lie in a heap. We should let him be a Jew of Palestine of nearly two thousand years ago; let him believe in the imminent end of the world and God's imminent judgment and, in prospect of that, call his hearers to a radical surrender to God. Only in so doing can we hope to discover the true "historical Jesus." We may even learn to appreciate him more.[2]

Yet some ethical pronouncements spoken by Jesus have stood the test of time. Particularly potent is his "Golden Rule" summary of the law of Moses and the Jewish prophets: "Do unto others as you would have them do unto you" (Matt 7:12). Ethicists rightly observe this Golden Rule is paralleled and applauded elsewhere. The book of Tobit, a work in the Old Testament Apocrypha, asserts the Golden Rule negatively (Tob 4:15), "What you hate, do to no man." John Stuart Mill, a founding father of utilitarian ethics, affirmed, "In the golden rule of Jesus of Nazareth, we read the complete spirit of the ethics of utility. To do as you

would be done by, and to love your neighbor as yourself, constitute the ideal perfection of utilitarian morality."[3] These parallels
are not surprising. What would be surprising, and troubling,
would be an absence of parallels to the Golden Rule in other
ethical systems.

I want us to turn now to a sixth question: Why did the Romans crucify Jesus? I want us to explore this matter because
comprehending Jesus' crucifixion from a historical viewpoint
undermines later theological attempts to understand Jesus' crucifixion as a sin sacrifice, a belief prominent in both Roman
Catholic and Protestant theology.

Notes

1. Charles Robert Darwin, *The Autobiography of Charles Darwin* (ed. Nora
Barlow; New York: W. W. Norton, 1958), 87.

2. Jack T. Sanders, *Ethics in the New Testament* (Philadelphia: Fortress Press
1975), 29.

3. John Stuart Mill, *Utilitarianism, On Liberty, Essay on Bentham* (Seattle:
Meridian Books, 1962), 268.

Chapter 6

Why Did the Romans
Crucify Jesus?

All four gospels report that Jesus spent the final days of his life in Jerusalem. He, along with supporters, traveled from Galilee to Jerusalem in order to observe a Jewish holiday called Passover. This holiday was a commemoration of the Jewish liberation from slavery and exodus out of Egypt in the time of Moses. There is a sense in which the Passover observance was to Jews what the Fourth of July is to Americans; both are celebrations of independence.

I want us to analyze in some detail an episode that took place at the beginning of Jesus' final Jerusalem visit. This episode is traditionally referred to as the "triumphal entry." This event is the stimulus for the church's observance (during Holy Week) of Palm Sunday. An analysis of the triumphal entry will go a long way, I believe, toward helping us understand why the Romans decided it was in their interest to get rid of Jesus.

Matthew's triumphal entry account reads as follows:

And when they drew near to Jerusalem and came to Bethphage, to the Mount of Olives, then Jesus sent two disciples, saying to them, "Go into the village opposite you, and immediately you will find an ass tied, and a colt with her; untie them and bring them to me. If any one says anything to you, you shall say, 'The Lord has need of them,' and he will send them immediately." This took place to fulfil what was spoken by the prophet, saying, "Tell the daughter of Zion, Behold, your king is coming to you, humble, and mounted

on an ass, and on a colt, the foal of an ass." The disciples went and did as Jesus had directed them; they brought
the ass and the colt, and put their garments on them, and
he sat thereon. Most of the crowd spread their garments
on the road, and others cut branches from the trees and
spread them on the road. And the crowds that went before him and that followed him shouted, "Hosanna to the
Son of David! Blessed is he who comes in the name of the
Lord! Hosanna in the highest!" And when he entered Jerusalem, all the city was stirred, saying "Who is this?" And
the crowds said, "This is the prophet Jesus from Nazareth
of Galilee." (Matt 21:1–11)

The other gospels provide additional details. John's gospel reports that the crowd of partisans accompanying Jesus (John
12:13) waved palm branches in the air. Luke's account has the
crowd proclaiming Jesus a king as they made their way into
Jerusalem. Luke 19:38 reports that the partisans shouted:

> "Blessed is the king
>   who comes in the name of the Lord!
> Peace in heaven,
>   and glory in the highest heaven!"

Normally, such an entry into Jerusalem might not attract the
eyes of the Roman governors. These governors did not spend
much time in Jerusalem. Ordinarily they stayed in delightful
Caesarea, just south of Carmel on the Mediterranean seacoast.
At Caesarea they could enjoy a cosmopolitan city with its harbor
made possible by massive stone moles jutting into the sea. They
could take pleasure in Mediterranean sea breezes while keeping
up with empire gossip garnered from travelers on ships sailing
from Rome across the eastern Mediterranean. Rarely did Roman
bureaucrats like Pontius Pilate spend time in provincial Jerusalem located high in the central hill country. To sophisticated
Romans it was a backward and curious city in the hinterlands.
    However, accompanied by armed soldiers, the Roman gover-

nors traveled regularly from Caesarea to Jerusalem during the Jewish Passover. The rationale for this Passover visit by the Roman authorities was to make certain Jewish behavior didn't "get out of hand." Scores of Jews resented Roman domination of their country. The Passover season, the Jewish Fourth of July, would be a tempting time for alienated Jews to express openly their hostility toward Rome. Thus Roman authorities came to Jerusalem during Passover to cope with possible seditious activity. While in Jerusalem the Romans stayed in the Tower of Antonia, a massive stone structure that was adjacent to the Jewish temple. Thus, since Pilate, governor of Palestine, had come to Jerusalem to monitor the Passover celebration, the stage was set for a conflict between Roman authorities and Jesus as he made his grand entry into the city.

To understand the Matthean account of the triumphal entry we must read it with Jewish eyes. Moreover, we must pay particular attention to Matt 21:5, which reads:

> Tell the daughter of Zion,
> Behold, your king is coming to you,
> humble, and mounted on an ass,
> and on a colt, the foal of an ass.

This verse is a quotation from Zechariah, a prophetic work in the Old Testament. Moreover, Zech 9:9 predicts that at some point in the future a king will come riding into Jerusalem on a donkey:

> Shout aloud, O daughter of Jerusalem!
> Lo, your king comes to you;
>   triumphant and victorious is he,
> humble and riding on an ass,
>   on a colt the foal of an ass.

During his final Jerusalem visit Jesus arrived at the Mount of Olives, a low hill immediately to the east of Jerusalem. He instructed his disciples to secure for him a donkey to ride on as he entered Jerusalem with his partisans. By so doing Jesus deliberately sought to fulfill or to act out the royal prophecy of

Zech 9:9. By so doing he was asserting he deemed himself to be king of the Jews.[1]

As Jesus rode into Jerusalem his partisans hailed him a king (Luke 19:38) and spread cloaks on the ground before him, an action suggestive of Jewish behavior when a person was designated a Jewish king (2 Kgs 9:13). Additionally, Jesus' admirers, according to John 12:13, waved palm branches in the air: "So they took branches of palm trees and went out to meet him, crying, 'Hosanna! Blessed be he who comes in the name of the Lord, even the king of Israel.' " This palm branch detail is not without significance. In Jewish thought the palm branch symbolized victory over one's enemies. Consider an episode recounted in 1 Maccabees, a Jewish historical work from the second century before the Christian era. Simon, one of the Maccabees, expelled unwanted Greek soldiers from the citadel, a structure in Jerusalem. After the expulsion of these detested Greek soldiers, Simon and his supporters entered the citadel with praise and palm branches. The Maccabean text continues:

> Those who were in the citadel at Jerusalem were prevented from going in and out to buy and sell in the country. So they were very hungry, and many of them perished from famine. Then they cried to Simon to make peace with them, and he did so. But he expelled them from there and cleansed the citadel from its pollution. On the twenty-third day of the second month, in the one hundred seventy-first year, the Jews entered it with praise and *palm branches,* and with harps and cymbals and stringed instruments, and with hymns and songs, because a great enemy had been crushed and removed from Israel. (1 Macc 13:49–51)

Another text suggesting that the palm branch symbolized victory is found in the Revelation, the last book of the New Testament. In Rev 7:9 a victorious heavenly host is described as being clothed in white robes while holding palm branches in their hands. "After this I looked, and behold, a great multitude which no man could number, from every nation, from all tribes and peoples and tongues, standing before the throne and before the Lamb, clothed in white robes, with palm branches in their hands." By waving palm branches during the triumphal entry, the Jesus partisans indicated that they were on the verge of experiencing victory over their enemies, the detested Romans.

Seeking to fulfill the royal prophecy of Zech 9:9, Jesus rode a donkey into Jerusalem at Passover. His partisans proclaimed him a king. They covered the ground with garments for him to ride over, waved palm branches (the Jewish "V for victory" sign) in the air, and shouted, "Blessed is the king who comes in the name of the Lord!" All of this in Roman eyes was seditious activity, broaching the possibility of revolt against the empire. The triumphal entry, I repeat, was Jesus' kiss of death in Roman eyes.

A short time later Pilate, working hand in glove with the Jewish religious elite who were upset over Jesus' cleansing of the temple, ordered Jesus to be crucified. On Jesus' cross a placard was nailed by Roman soldiers spelling out the reason for the execution. The placard read: King of the Jews. Thus Jesus was executed for treason against Rome. His crucifixion was a feral yet understandable act of bureaucratic brutality. In all likelihood Pilate and the soldiers didn't give Jesus' crucifixion a second thought. In their eyes his execution was "all in a day's work." They were disposing of a troublemaker. "The Galilean prophet got what he asked for. He should have had better sense than to fool around with Rome." Understanding Jesus' execution from this historical perspective undercuts subsequent attempts by theologians to build "atonement theories" on his crucifixion. Theologians contend Jesus' death was a sacrifice for sin. One is hard-pressed to discover evidence suggesting Jesus viewed his death as a sacrifice for mankind's sinfulness.

Notes

1. Parenthetically, Matthew's account of the triumphal entry (contra the other gospels) states that Jesus (like a circus rider) rode *two animals* into Jerusalem. The text (Matt 21:7) reads: "they brought the ass and the colt, and put their garments on them, and he sat thereon." This grotesque two-animal

assertion reveals the gospel writer did not understand what is referred to in poetry as a synonymous parallelism. A synonymous parallelism is a poetic device wherein the *same idea* is sequentially expressed in *two different ways*. Psalm 19:1 contains a well-known synonymous parallelism: "The heavens declare the glory of God and the firmament shows his handiwork." Firmament is simply another term for *heavens*. Thus the psalmist is expressing the same idea in two different ways: the heavens (i.e., firmament) reveal God's creative greatness. Zech 9:9 contains a synonymous parallelism involving an "ass" and the "foal (young) of an ass." The prediction asserts that a king will some day ride into Jerusalem on an ass (i.e., a colt, the foal of an ass). This predictions says the *same thing* in two different ways, but Matthew interpreted this synonymous parallelism literally and curiously portrays Jesus riding two animals simultaneously. The triumphal-entry accounts in Mark 11:1–10, Luke 19:29–38, and John 12:12–19 report that Jesus rode one animal (not two) into Jerusalem.

Chapter 7

In Conclusion

On previous pages we have grappled with six questions that can be asked concerning the historical Jesus. What was his major message? What was his attitude toward Gentiles? What were the circumstances surrounding his birth? What did Jesus think about God? What were his ethical teachings? Why did the Romans crucify him?

By no means do these questions exhaust all issues that could be explored concerning the historical Jesus. For example, in our discussion, no attention has been paid to his parables. No notice has been given to his conflicts with Pharisees and Sadducees. No consideration has been given to Jesus' role as a healer. I have no difficulty believing Jesus healed sick people. Why? Convincing accounts exist of other healers — both past and present — who possess curative powers.[1] If they can heal, why not Jesus? His ability to heal goes a long way toward explaining his popularity with ordinary people. Jews living in the first century knew nothing of modern medicines and hospitals. Thus common folk were elated over Jesus' ability to heal the lame, the blind, and the deaf.

In a word, much Jesus material has been left out of our discussion. This excluded data tends to be material over which Jesus scholars do not disagree. Having acknowledged this omission, however, I contend the six questions discussed above bring into focus some of the problematic issues the church has tended to ignore for two thousand years. The church curiously has downplayed or de-emphasized the very dimensions of Jesus' life and teachings that make him understandable as a historical person. Heeding the six just-discussed questions, I propose we now summarize Jesus' life as partially understood by post-Enlightenment scholarship.

A Brief Post-Enlightenment Account of Jesus' Life

Two thousand years ago a Jew named Jesus was born on the eastern fringe of the Roman Empire. He was the biological son of a Jewish mother named Mary and a Jewish father named Joseph. Jesus' birth was irregular, but today the precise nature of that irregularity cannot be determined.

Little is known about Jesus' youth. Around thirty years of age he submitted to the water and repentance baptism of John the baptizer, a wilderness prophet who was calling Jews to repentance and was announcing the imminent coming of the kingdom of God (Matt 3:2). Jesus adopted John the baptizer's message and began proclaiming that the grand finale of history was at hand. The God of Abraham was about to interrupt human affairs and provide to repenting Jews a utopian kingdom. In this utopian realm Jesus would be God's viceroy, and the twelve Jewish tribes would be reconstituted to be ruled by Jesus' primary disciples. Passover would be observed. A banquet would be enjoyed by the kingdom's participants. Entry into the kingdom would be through a narrow door supervised by Jesus. The door's keys would be entrusted to Peter.

Jesus told parables to illuminate this kingdom. He compared the kingdom to a pearl of great price, to a hidden treasure, and to a mustard seed that grows into the greatest of all shrubs.

Jesus sent disciples out to announce the good news (the gospel) that this kingdom was soon to appear. He instructed them to go only to the lost sheep of the house of Israel. This gospel was not for Gentiles, whom Jesus viewed as dogs and pigs.

Jesus believed the kingdom's arrival would be accompanied by celestial fireworks. The sun would be darkened, the moon would no longer give its light, and stars would fall from heaven (Mark 13:24–25). A mysterious Son of Man would descend on heavenly clouds and send out angels to gather the elect. This Son of Man would sit on a throne and judge mankind, paying attention to how people had treated the hungry, thirsty, and strangers (Matt 25:31–46). Those who did not pass the hungry-thirsty-stranger test would be doomed to eternal fire prepared for the devil and his angels (Matt 25:41) while those who did pass would be ushered into eternal life (Matt 25:46).

To announce and to warn that the kingdom was about to appear was the rationale for Jesus' public ministry. Yet this kingdom did not appear. What Jesus expected to happen did not happen. Thus the ministry of Jesus was predicated on a mistake.

Jesus was a thaumaturge endowed with therapeutic healing power. He was also a moral teacher. As such, he was immersed in the law (Torah) of Moses. He articulated behavior norms like the Golden Rule. He also expressed behavior norms that are impossible for people who live pedestrian lives to observe. For example, "Give to him who begs from you, and do not refuse him who would borrow from you." Or, "Do not lay up for yourselves treasures on earth." Such behavior norms are simultaneously admired and ignored by most of Jesus' disciples. While a moral teacher, Jesus deliberately associated with society's riffraff, gaining the reputation of being a glutton and drunkard (Luke 7:34).

At the end of his life Jesus journeyed to Jerusalem to observe Passover. On this final visit he antagonized the Jewish religious elite by leading a temple revolt. He upset Roman authorities by presenting himself to his contemporaries as a king. The Romans executed Jesus because in their eyes he was a rebel against the empire.

Finally, Jesus did not deem himself to be God. Instead, as a devout Jew he prayed to God and ended his life with the poignant cry, "My God, my God, why have you forsaken me?"

Orthodox Christianity does not agree with this partial reconstruction of Jesus' life and thought as posited by post-Enlightenment scholarship. This disagreement is not surprising. Orthodox Christians are loaded down with heavy belief baggage consisting of distortions, pious exaggerations, and well-intentioned falsehoods promulgated over the years in sermons, hymns, and confessions of faith. Be that as it may, I propose we now (taking into account the six questions just discussed) summarize the life of Jesus as partially understood by orthodox Christianity.

A Brief Orthodox Account of Jesus' Life

Two thousand years ago a Jew named Jesus was born on the eastern fringe of the Roman Empire. Born to a holy virgin, Jesus was God in human form. Those who saw him either as an infant or as an adult were looking at God the Son, one of the blessed Trinity. Jesus was a religious teacher who proclaimed the coming of the kingdom of God. This kingdom was inaugurated by Jesus and continues today as the church and as the rule of God in human hearts. Living a sinless life, Jesus was a superb moral teacher. His disciples — living two millennia later — can walk 'in his steps' by applying his ethical teachings in their everyday lives. Jesus loved everybody (both Jews and Gentiles). He evidenced this comprehensive love by dying on a Roman cross as a sacrifice for mankind's sins. Indeed, the major reason Jesus came from heaven to earth was to provide a sacrificial means by which sinners can be forgiven from their transgressions.

These two understandings of Jesus' life are as different as night and day. Both cannot be right. Consequently, the Christian movement today is suffering from theological-ideological schizophrenia. Christian theology is a house divided. On the one hand, some Christian thinkers believe the church must take into account post-Enlightenment scholarship and the historical Jesus. Christians of this genre are called (at least in some circles) "liberals." They view post-Enlightenment scholarship embodied in the historical-critical method as a new way of doing theology. To them it is a new instrument to make sense out of the Christian faith. As Hans Küng observed, "With the historical-critical method . . . theology is provided with an instrument enabling the question about the true, real, historical Christ to be asked in a way that was simply not possible in former centuries."[2]

On the other hand, theologians devoted to orthodox Christianity believe emphasis should be placed on the church's revered doctrines and dogmas. They accept without reservations the conclusions reached centuries ago by the great ecumenical councils of the church and the beliefs embodied in the church's creeds. To them the Christian faith is a complex of doctrinal gems that should be passed on from one generation of believers to the next. Indeed, some theologians view the historical Jesus and life-of-Jesus research as irrelevant to the Christian faith. Over the years Christian thinkers as diverse as Anselm, Thomas Aquinas, John Calvin, Sören Kierkegaard, Paul Tillich, Karl Barth, and Emil Brunner have been indifferent to the historical Jesus. So is the Reverend Billy Graham, America's foremost evangelist. I once heard the Reverend Graham remark in a sermon, "If it could be demonstrated tomorrow that Jesus never lived, I would continue being a Christian because being a Christian is so much fun." Martin Kähler, late professor of systematic theology at the University of Halle, contended that all he needed to know about Jesus was that he died for our sins, was buried, and was raised on the third day. He observed, "If I have all this, I do not need additional information on the precise details of Jesus' life and death."[3] Not surprisingly, some Christian thinkers of this genre go so far as to view the historical Jesus as a burden or pain. Karl Rahner, late Jesuit theologian of Munich, observed in his *Foundations of Christian Faith*, "Today Jesus Christ is himself a problem."[4] This remark is similar to one made by Karl Barth, "The Lord Jesus is a problem child (*Sorgenkind*) to the theologian, a problem child that ought throughout to be accorded respect and that somehow does receive respect, but a problem child nevertheless."[5]

Ordinary sitting-on-the-pew Christians are not bothered by this liberal-orthodox disagreement. They have never heard of Johannes Weiss or Albert Schweitzer or life-of-Jesus research and could care less. Ordinary Christians in the part of the country where I live, the deep south, do not think their religion; they sing their religion. A religious belief embedded in a familiar gospel hymn is never questioned.

Two groups, however, are negatively affected by the conflict between post-Enlightenment scholarship and entrenched orthodox Christianity. One group negatively affected are members of the clergy who received their theological training at seminaries where they were exposed to contemporary biblical scholarship (the kind of scholarship encountered at schools like Emory University in Atlanta and the Harvard Divinity School in Cambridge). Before attending seminaries they innocently assumed there was an obvious or normative Christian gospel. But after acquiring a seminary education, they ponder the question: What is the gospel? Discombobulated, they spend their entire professional lives in a quandary. They slip and slide when expounding the kingdom of God to their parishioners. In this regard they resemble pigs dancing on ice. While preaching on race relationships, they circumvent Jesus' opinion that Gentiles are dogs. While preaching about Jesus dying on the cross as a sacrifice for mankind's sins, they inwardly grope for an atonement theory that would make sense out of what they proclaim. Their mouths and minds are not connected. Unsure of what the gospel is, these pastors employ gospel substitutes. The primary gospel substitute in our day is pastoral counseling. In sermons they advise parishioners on how to get along with teenage daughters. They preach homilies on how to conquer inferiority complexes.

Another group negatively affected by the conflict between post-Enlightenment scholarship and entrenched orthodoxy are inquisitive lay persons. Thomas F. O'Dea in his book on Mormonism observed that the only unhappy Mormons are those who think. Similarly, the only unhappy lay Christians are those who reflect. They sense something is wrong with their Christian belief system, but they don't know what it is. Some walk away from the church with a "well-I-tried" attitude. Others stay but are haunted by a feeling of discontent.

I believe the danger confronting contemporary Christianity is the rejection, or ignoring, of post-Enlightenment scholarship and the embalming of the message about Jesus in a doctrinal belief system that no longer "rings the bell" of inquisitive believers. Inquisitive believers, alas, are unwilling to accept the simplistic definition of faith as believing that which you know is not true.

Can Jesus be rescued from the church's dogmatic castle where many Christians believe he should remain ensconced? Is there a solution to the church's schizophrenia of mind versus dogma? Is it possible to be a Christian believer without committing intellectual suicide?

Notes

1. Any person interested in reading about miraculous healings should read John G. Fuller's *Arigo: Surgeon of the Rusty Knife* (New York: Pocket Books, 1975). Arigo was a Brazilian peasant who lived in a remote village named Congonhas do Campo. People in droves came to him to be healed. A devout Roman Catholic, Arigo slashed his patients with rusty knives, used no anesthetics, and confounded the world with thousands of miraculous cures. Tragically he was killed in an automobile accident. In the October 16, 1972, issue of *Time* magazine the following statement appeared concerning Arigo:

> Even before he died last year in an automobile accident at the age of 49, the peasant known as Arigo had become a legend in his native Brazil. Claiming to be guided by the wise voice of a long-deceased physician whom he had never known personally, the uneducated healer saw as many as 300 patients a day, diagnosing and treating them in minutes.... He treated almost every known ailment, and most of his patients not only survived but actually improved or recovered. A few years ago, reports on the exploits of such miracle workers would have drawn little more than derision from the scientifically-trained. Now, however, many medical researchers are showing a new open-mindedness toward so-called psychic healing and other methods not taught in medical schools.

2. Küng, *On Being a Christian* (New York: Doubleday, 1976), 156.

3. Kähler, *The So-Called Historical Jesus,* 60.

4. Karl Rahner, *Foundations of Christian Faith* (London: Seabury, 1978), 13.

5. This Barth quotation is in Jaroslav Pelikan, *Jesus through the Centuries* (New Haven: Yale University Press, 1985), 201. This book should be read by every inquisitive Christian. Pelikan shows how across the centuries the church has had a kaleidoscopic understanding of Jesus. Charles Guignebert, late professor of the history of Christianity in the Sorbonne, in his book on Jesus' life quoted Albert Schweitzer as saying, "We must be prepared to find that the

historical knowledge of the personality of Jesus will not be a help, but perhaps even an offense to religion." Guignebert continues, "When Schweitzer then goes on to speak of the grotesque, repellent, and startling figure that might very well confront us if an attempt at historical reconstruction were conceivably to be successful, we are bound to sympathize with the despair that must arise in the heart of any fairminded theologian who penetrates into the sources of his faith. Schweitzer's *The Quest of the Historic Jesus* . . . ends up on the note of hopelessness . . . at the irreconcilability of Jesus' outlook with that of the whole of organized Christianity since. This is a contradiction which no apologetics can palliate or bypass." See p. xiii in *Jesus* by Charles Guignebert published in 1956 by University Books of New York.

Part Two

Four Strategies for Rescuing Jesus

Inquisitive believers confront a dilemma. Sympathetic to post-Enlightenment scholarship, wanting to be intellectually honest with the data, they are aware of the gulf separating the historical Jesus from the embellished Jesus encountered in the creeds and dogmas of the church. For example, personal integrity keeps them from believing Jesus was an "infallible, omniscient teacher" who viewed himself as being God. Yet they are aware that orthodox Christianity views Jesus as God the Son who as an "infallible, omniscient teacher" proclaimed a "perfect" message to his hearers of two thousand years ago. Moreover, inquisitive believers are aware that the vast majority of Christians would be appalled if they knew of Albert Schweitzer's contention that Jesus was a mistaken prophet. A majority of Christians rejoice in the orthodox "old time religion," which they view as their ticket to heaven. They cannot tolerate their beliefs being questioned or disturbed. I shall never forget a remark made to me years ago by a Mississippi delta plantation owner: "Take orthodoxy away from common people and you transform them into atheists."

So what are inquisitive believers to do? Should they say "to heck with it" and walk away from the Christian faith? Should they sullenly submit to mainstream Christianity, thereby succumbing to what John Stuart Mill called "the tyranny of the majority"? Or should they follow the advice given to Alice in

71

Alice in Wonderland? The Queen stated she was a hundred and one years, five months and one day old. Alice responded, "I can't believe that." "Can't you?" said the Queen. "Try again. Draw a deep breath and shut your eyes." Is shutting your eyes and drawing a deep breath a workable alternative?

None of these alternatives works satisfactorily. Instead, I shall suggest four strategies for inquisitive believers to use whereby Jesus can be rescued from orthodox Christians who have imprisoned him in a belief system that since the Enlightenment has become less and less plausible. I am using the term "strategy" in the sense of a plan or a method by which to achieve some goal. My goal is to provide reflective believers with a method or procedure by which they can be Christians with a sense of integrity. I am not arguing that an inquisitive Christianity that strives for intellectual honesty is in itself "superior" to orthodox Christianity. I am contending, however, that it is an alternative, valid version of the Christian faith.

The first of the four strategies I shall discuss concerns the resurrection. This strategy, like the other three, presupposes theism and the view that God was active in the Christ event.

Chapter 8

Strategy One

*Distinguish between the Pre-Resurrection Jesus
and the Post-Resurrection Jesus*

Inquisitive believers, as a first step, can begin rescuing Jesus by perceiving and taking seriously the difference between the pre-resurrection and the post-resurrection Jesus. Although related, they are not the same. A recognition of this difference can go a long way toward helping believers "make sense" out of the Christian faith.

Biblical scholars agree that early on a Friday, 15 Nisan, Jesus and two other men, described in the Gospels as "robbers," were taken outside Jerusalem, were nailed to crosses by Roman soldiers, and were left on these crosses to die. Jesus and the two robbers were not the only men in the first century crucified by Roman soldiers. Scores of other Jews were crucified also. During the first-century Jewish revolt against the Roman Empire, the Romans crucified many Jews for treason against the empire. Flavius Josephus, a Jewish historian, wrote an account of these crucifixions. His account is similar to the New Testament account of Jesus' maltreatment by the Romans:

> So they (the Roman soldiers) first whipped (the Jews) and then tormented them with all sorts of tortures. . . . The soldiers, out of the wrath and hatred they bore the Jews, nailed those they caught, one after one way, and another after another, to the crosses, by way of jest, when their multitude was so great, that room was wanting for the crosses, and crosses wanting for the bodies. (*Jewish War* V, 11, 1)

73

Jesus died toward nightfall immediately before the Sabbath began. Joseph of Arimathea, a Jew looking for the kingdom of God (Mark 15:43), went to Pilate and asked for Jesus' corpse. His request was granted. Joseph bought a linen cloth, removed Jesus' corpse from the cross, and placed the shroud-wrapped corpse in a rock-hewn tomb. This crucifixion was the final event in the human life of the historical Jesus.

But Jesus' story does not end with his death and burial. A day and a half after the crucifixion some women went to the tomb to anoint Jesus' body. They found the tomb empty. To their surprise and dismay, Jesus appeared to them. He appeared later to his disciples. In Christian thought these post-burial Christ appearances are collectively referred to as the resurrection.

With reference to the resurrection, I want us to consider the following questions. Is it plausible to believe Jesus was raised from the dead? Assuming the resurrection occurred, is the pre-resurrection Jesus identical with the post-resurrection Jesus? Unfortunately, I shall argue, in Christian thought the pre-resurrection Jesus and the post-resurrection Jesus have been unwisely blended.

Before discussing the plausibility question, however, I would like to make three preliminary observations.

First, in the Gospels Jesus' resurrection is not explicitly described. There are no human eyewitnesses to the resurrection. No Jesus partisan is reported to have said, "I was inside the tomb when the resurrection took place, and I can describe and explain to you what happened." Post-resurrection appearances are reported but not the resurrection itself.

Second, early Christian literature does not suggest Jesus rose from the dead by his own power. Instead, in New Testament thought Jesus' resurrection is viewed as a deed or accomplishment of God. For example, on the day of Pentecost Peter asserted:

Men of Israel, hear these words: Jesus of Nazareth, a man attested to you by God with mighty works and wonders and signs which God did through him in your midst . . . you crucified and killed by the hands of lawless men. But God raised him up, having loosed the pangs of death, because it was not possible for him to be held by it. (Acts 2:22–24)

"But God raised him up!" Paul could write these same words to the Thessalonian Christians and refer to the "living and true God" as the one who raised Jesus "from the dead" (1 Thess 1:9–10).

Third, Jesus' resurrection appearances were made exclusively to Jews. No reference is made of a resurrection appearance to Gentiles.

From time to time believers and skeptics have debated questions such as: Was Jesus raised from the dead? Can Jesus' resurrection be proven? Such questions are booby traps. They fail to consider the limitations of human knowledge. They do not recognize the limits of historical inquiry. The only people who could "prove beyond a shadow of doubt" that Jesus was resurrected are witnesses of two millennia ago who saw and heard and encountered the resurrected Jesus. This option is impossible for us. Indeed, there is no way "to prove" conclusively or empirically any past event. The terms "prove" and "proof" are verbal abstractions and have caused much woe and discord in theological discussions.

Historical knowledge by its very nature is limited. Past events cannot be reconstructed or re-enacted or re-witnessed. Consequently, when discussing a past event the best we can do is speak in terms of plausibility and probability. Did a given past event probably occur? Is it plausible to believe a given past event took place? This plausible-probable alternative is recognized by New Testament scholars such as Luke Timothy Johnson of Emory University and historians such as the late Carl Becker of Cornell University. According to Johnson, for example,

What is most important, however, is that the serious historian knows and acknowledges that historical knowledge deals only in degrees of probability, and never with certainty.

The best historians candidly acknowledge their inability to penetrate the "reality" of the past, and confess that their craft involves in equal measure the attempt to verify the remaining evidence and the willingness to exercise creative guesswork to supply the most *plausible* or *probable* version that the evidence allows.[1]

In a similar vein the historian Carl Becker observed that in dealing with any past event the historian

cannot deal directly with (the) event itself, since the event itself has disappeared. What he can deal with directly is a *statement about the event*. He deals in short not with the event, but with a statement which affirms *the fact that the event occurred*. When we really get down to the hard facts, what the historian is always dealing with is an *affirmation* — an affirmation of the fact that something is true. There is thus a distinction of capital importance to be made: the distinction between the ephemeral event which disappears, and the affirmation about the event which persists.[2]

Thus assuming Jesus was raised from the dead, we must concede that his actual resurrection has disappeared and is irretrievable for investigation. Christian apologists put themselves over a barrel when they accept the challenge: "prove Jesus' resurrection occurred." You cannot prove a no-longer-existing event. What the church does have, however, are affirmations, written accounts, of the resurrection. Our earliest accounts are found in 1 Cor 15:1–11 and in the four gospels. The four gospels are by far the best preserved manuscripts that have come down to us from the ancient world of two thousand years ago. Monasteries (like the Monastery of St. Catherine at the base of Mt. Sinai), libraries (like the Vatican Library in Rome), and museums (like the British Museum in London) have scores of early gospel manuscripts. The early Christian movement produced a literary explosion. This literary explosion suggests "something" must have happened that was the stimulus for this explosion.

Since Jesus' resurrection cannot be proven, is it plausible to believe Jesus was resurrected from the dead and appeared to his disciples in a manner they found to be convincing? There are no events other than the resurrection and the disciples' fervent belief in the resurrection that can explain the Christian religion's explosive emergence two millennia ago on the eastern fringe of the Roman Empire. From a human viewpoint Jesus was no Jewish Napoleon or Alexander the Great. Instead, from a human viewpoint Jesus was insignificant. Others have observed that he never traveled more than ninety miles from the place of his birth. He never visited a major city in the Roman Empire. He led no armies and conquered no territory. He wrote no books. He spent a considerable part of his life in microscopic villages like Nazareth and Capernaum. He was not a person of wealth. He lived as a Jew among Jews, an ethnic cluster despised by sophisticates of that day. His recorded words can be read in about an hour's time and his main message turned out to be a mistake. At the end of his life he was crucified between thieves and was buried in a borrowed tomb. Common sense suggests that after his death this insignificant and mistaken man should have been forgotten — lost in what C. P. Snow called "the sludge" of human history. Yet shortly after the crucifixion his disciples (who previously had fled out of fear, sadness, and disappointment and who are described by Pinchas Lapide as "Galilean hillbillies") were transformed into a rejoicing community of believers and began proclaiming that Jesus was lord and would soon return on clouds of glory. Against overwhelming odds the religion emanating from Jesus displaced the established religions of the empire.

Why did the Christian movement begin as and when it did? What was the stimulus that overnight transformed Jesus' disciples into a rejoicing community and propelled the Christian faith into existence? The plausible answer: the resurrection. Any skeptic who denies the resurrection is under obligation to posit a reason other than the resurrection for the disciples' post-crucifixion behavior and the Christian religion's emergence and dynamic growth. I know of no alternative explanation that is plausible.

Moreover, a person who denies the resurrection in itself is forced to view the resurrection accounts in the Gospels as fraudulent. This "fraud" view entails difficulties. For example, assuming the resurrection accounts are deceitful, how does one explain the skepticism motif that permeates them? Would not a fraudulent, deceiving account have asserted boastfully: "There is no doubt about it! Jesus' disciples unreservedly know the resurrection occurred. The evidence is overwhelming and undeniable!" Instead, the resurrection accounts in the Gospels have an overlay of skepticism. Matthew asserts that some of the apostles doubted the resurrection even after the appearance of the risen Jesus in Galilee (Matt 28:17). The longer ending to Mark's gospel states that after the resurrection Jesus "appeared to the eleven themselves as they sat at table; and he upbraided them for their unbelief and hardness of heart, because they had not believed those who saw him after he had risen" (Mark 16:14). Luke's gospel tells of Mary Magdalene, Joanna, and Mary the mother of James reporting to the apostles their discovery of the empty tomb. What was the reaction of the apostles to this feminine report? "These words seemed to them an idle tale, and they did not believe them" (Luke 24:11).

Assuming the resurrection accounts are deceitful, how does one explain the limitation of the resurrection appearances to Jews? Only Jews saw and conversed with the risen Jesus. Would not fraudulent, deceiving accounts have asserted: "The risen Jesus appeared to multitudes — both Jews and Gentiles. He taunted Pilate and the Roman soldiers who crucified him by appearing to them as risen lord. His resurrection appearances were as numerous as they were irrefutable!" To the contrary, the resurrection accounts are characterized by reserve.

Assuming the resurrection accounts are fraudulent, why did the early Christian community go to the trouble of adopting the first day of the week (Sunday: the resurrection day) as a day of worship? Were the early "deceiving" Christians so naive as to think a day of worship other than the Sabbath would beguile others and aid in their program of deception? Moreover, what would have been the perverse motivation for the early Christian community to deceive itself and to deceive others by fabricating a "poppycock" resurrection story? If the early Christians knew the resurrection accounts were "poppycock," why didn't they apostatize when persecution broke out against them? The emergence of the Christian movement establishes the plausibility of the resurrection.

Having contended belief in the resurrection is plausible, I want to consider the second question previously posed: assuming the resurrection occurred, is the pre-resurrection Jesus identical to the post-resurrection Jesus?[3]

Some readers may consider this distinction to be theological hair-splitting that has no useful religious significance for contemporary Christians. But the church's failure across the centuries to distinguish between the pre-resurrection Jesus and the post-resurrection Jesus has made it impossible for Christians to have a realistic understanding of the historical Jesus. The church, unfortunately, has blended the pre-Easter Jesus and the post-Easter Jesus into a homogenized whole. As a result of this blending the historical Jesus has been weighted down with a dogmatic overload foreclosing honest life-of-Jesus research. Moreover, I insist that the pre-Easter Jesus and the post-Easter Jesus are both important. Without the historical Jesus the post-resurrection Jesus would be an ideological mannequin. Inquisitive Christians can rescue Jesus from the creedal prison in which he now resides by distinguishing in their own minds between the pre-Easter Jesus and the post-Easter Jesus.

The distinction between the pre-Easter and post-Easter Jesus appears in the New Testament. In his introduction to Romans, Paul differentiated between, on the one hand, the Jesus who was "descended from David according to the flesh" and, on the other hand, the Jesus who was "designated Son of God in power according to the Spirit of holiness by his resurrection from the dead" (Rom 1:1–4). Thus there was the "flesh" Jesus and the "Son of God" Jesus.

The pre-Easter Jesus was born around 4 B.C.E. and was executed by the Romans around 30 C.E. He was a man with a body of flesh, bone, and blood. Living at Capernaum by the Sea of Galilee, he expounded the Mosaic law, told parables, healed the sick, associated with sinners, and debated Pharisees and Sadducees. As a Galilean Jew he believed a marvelous kingdom of God was about to arrive on earth. This kingdom would be a Jewish haven. Accounts of his life, which can be studied and evaluated by historians, exist in early Christian literature. This historical Jesus of flesh and blood, however, no longer exists. Like Socrates or Aristotle, the historical Jesus is a human figure of the past.

The expression "post-resurrection Jesus" refers to Jesus after he was raised from the dead and began appearing to his disciples. Whereas the historical Jesus has ceased to exist, the post-resurrection Jesus continues to exist to the present day. To try to define or to describe the risen Jesus is a problematical endeavor. Likewise, to try to analyze his resurrection appearances is problematical. Both are mysteries; by their very nature mysteries cannot be explained. If they could be explained, they would not be mysteries. These resurrection encounters, which are recounted in the New Testament, were not "inner, subjective experiences" or hallucinations experienced by the disciples. Rather these resurrection encounters were empirical in nature. The disciples "saw" and "heard" the resurrected Jesus. Thus in early Christian thought the name "Jesus" has two denotations or referents: the historical, pre-resurrection Jesus and the suprahistorical, post-resurrection Jesus.[4] Although these referents are related, they are not identical.

In seeking to reflect on the post-resurrection Jesus we again must realize we are entering a contested territory. Human knowledge is limited; some matters we cannot completely understand. The precise identity of either the pre-resurrection or the post-resurrection Jesus is one of those matters. But what can be said is: for two thousand years the post-resurrection Jesus has flourished in the realm of religion as a magnetic, evocative figure. Scores of people, from a St. Francis to a Dwight L. Moody to a Mother Teresa, have found themselves fascinated by him and drawn to him. Such is the case because God impinges on their religious intuitions and authenticates or confirms Jesus as a person of religious significance. The post-resurrection Jesus provides them with a moral-behavior motive and with the hope of a blessed future life. His resurrection confirms there is a mode of existence beyond death.

But some orthodox Christians, alas, make mistakes in regard to the post-resurrection Jesus. They repeatedly view the post-resurrection Jesus through a rearview mirror. They think of the resurrected Jesus as one who appeared to his disciples for a brief time after his resurrection but has, for all practical purposes, disappeared. As far as they are concerned, the post-resurrection Jesus is as much a figure of the past as the pre-resurrection Jesus is a figure of the past. They fail to realize that the resurrected Jesus lives today in the spirit world, or the realm of religious experience, and impinges upon people's lives as a pulsating religious stimulus.

Moreover, orthodox Christians blend or homogenize the pre-resurrection Jesus and the post-resurrection Jesus. In their minds the two are the same. Jesus on "this side" of the resurrection is the same as Jesus on the "other side" of the resurrection. They go further and take dogmas developed by the church (such as Jesus is God the Son, one of the blessed Trinity) and retroject (thrust backward) those dogmas upon the historical Jesus. This retrojection befuddles their understanding of the historical Jesus. They reason as follows: "Jesus could not have been mistaken about the imminent arrival of the kingdom of God because he was God and God does not make mistakes." Or, "Jesus could not have uttered dubious moral teachings because he was God and God is morally perfect." Or, "Jesus could not have had a negative attitude toward Gentiles because he was God and God loves everybody." This way of reasoning has transformed

the historical Jesus into God incognito. The blending of the pre-
and post-resurrection Jesus goes a long way toward explaining
why orthodox Christians resent the post-Enlightenment quest
for the historical Jesus. This quest has upturned aspects of Jesus'
life and thought, such as his mistaken belief about the kingdom's imminence, which cannot be harmonized with orthodox
Christianity's conception of Jesus as God incognito.

Inquisitive Christians need not and should not blend the pre-
Easter Jesus with the post-Easter Jesus. Inquisitive Christians
should keep them separate in their minds. They can believe both
in a fallible, human historical Jesus and in a charismatic, post-
Easter Jesus. Such is the case because a life can have more than
one stage or chapter. I shall illustrate what I mean by citing Abraham Lincoln. One stage in his life could be called the pre-1860
stage (his life before being elected this country's sixteenth president); a second stage in his life could be called the post-1860
stage (his life after being elected president). In many ways the
first stage of Lincoln's life was as difficult as it was unpromising.
He was born in 1809 in a log cabin located some five miles south
of Elizabethtown, Kentucky. His father — Thomas Lincoln — was
compelled to move from Kentucky to Indiana because of trouble over property rights. In Indiana Lincoln's mother died from
"milk sickness." Seeking a better life, the Lincoln family move
to New Salem, Illinois. During all this time Abraham Lincoln received less than a year of formal education. As a young man he
ran for the state legislature of Illinois and was defeated. He then
bought a store in New Salem and within a matter of months
went bankrupt. He spent years paying off bad debts from this
mercantile venture. Lincoln asked Mary Owens, a Kentucky girl
visiting her sister who lived in New Salem, to marry him; she rejected his proposal. While practicing law (a profession he taught
himself) he sought on two occasions the Whig nomination for
Congress from his district in Illinois; he was denied both nom-
inations. In 1858 he ran for the United States Senate and was
defeated by Stephen A. Douglas. Finally, in 1860 at the age of
fifty-two, Lincoln was elected president of the United States.

This presidential election marks the beginning of a second stage in Lincoln's life: the post-1860 stage. During this stage the Civil War was fought. Lincoln is remembered as the president who freed the slaves and preserved the union. His Gettysburg Address has become an American classic. Today the Mall in Washington is dominated by the Lincoln Memorial, a marble structure that is a reminder that Abraham Lincoln was a noble president who led this country through the agony of the Civil War.

Does any aspect of Lincoln's pre-1860 stage-in-life nullify or belittle any aspect of his post-1860 stage-in-life? Did going bankrupt as a merchant in New Salem, Illinois nullify Lincoln's Gettysburg Address? Did being defeated by Stephen A. Douglas in an 1858 senatorial campaign nullify Lincoln's election to the presidency in 1860? Did Lincoln's lack of formal education diminish his role as the president who saved the union? All of these questions should be answered in the negative. One truth does not nullify or diminish or destroy another truth.

This line of reasoning can be applied to the two stages of Jesus' life: the historical, pre-resurrection Jesus and the suprahistorical, post-resurrection Jesus. Does his mistake about the imminent arrival of the kingdom of God, his negative attitude toward Gentiles, his at-times impractical ethical teachings, and his savage crucifixion nullify his resurrection from the dead, his appearances to his disciples, and his continuing influence on mankind? Does his possibly irregular birth (was Mary a Jewish prostitute who gave birth to Jesus out of wedlock?) destroy his central role in a religion with some two billion adherents? Questions like these should be answered in the negative. Again I emphasize: one truth does not nullify or diminish or destroy another truth.

Inquisitive Christians should hold the post-resurrection Jesus in esteem while at the same time accepting the limitations of the historical, pre-resurrection Jesus. Both conceptions of Jesus are important. Without the historical Jesus the post-Easter Jesus would be like a mannequin or a marble statue in a European museum. Moreover, the reality and potency of the post-resurrection

Jesus implies that Christians have nothing to fear from conclusions reached by Enlightenment and post-Enlightenment
investigation into the thought and deeds of the historical Jesus.
Such is the case because the resurrected Jesus exists indepen-
dently of scholarly investigation of the historical Jesus. However,
believers can place so much emphasis on Jesus that he displaces
God and, consequently, the Christian religion degenerates into a
sentimental Jesus cult.

Notes

1. Luke Timothy Johnson, *The Real Jesus* (San Francisco: HarperSan-
Francisco, 1996), 85. Every person interested in life-of-Jesus research should
read Professor Johnson's book, in which he gives attention to the historical
puzzle of origination. Why did the Christian movement originate some two
thousand years ago? What was the stimulus for its appearance on the world
scene? Professor Johnson cogently argues that Jesus' resurrection and continuing influence as risen and living Christ is the reason for the Christian
movement's "unlikely birth" and "amazing growth."

2. This distinction between past events, which have disappeared, and writ-
ten accounts of those disappeared events appears in Carl Becker, "What Are
Historical Facts?," in *The Philosophy of History in Our Time* (ed. Hans Meyerhoff;
New York: Doubleday Anchor Books, 1959), 124.

3. At this point I acknowledge my indebtedness to Marcus Borg, prolific
author and religion professor at Oregon State University. To my knowledge no
other New Testament scholar has done as much as Professor Borg to hammer
home the distinction that should be made between the pre-Easter Jesus and
the post-Easter Jesus, or the distinction between the historical Jesus and the
Jesus of Christian orthodoxy.

4. Marcus Borg, "From Galilean Jew to the Face of God: The Pre-Easter and
Post-Easter Jesus," in *Jesus at 2000* (ed. Marcus Borg; Boulder, Colo.: Westview
Press, 1998), 8.

Chapter 9

Strategy Two

No Obligation Exists to Accept All Beliefs
Held by the Early Church

One strategy inquisitive believers can employ to rescue Jesus from orthodox Christians is to distinguish between the pre-resurrection Jesus and the post-resurrection Jesus. I want us now to consider a second strategy: reflective Christians should realize they are not obligated to believe everything early Christians believed. The statute of limitations applies also to religious beliefs. The early church held some beliefs that are today untenable.

Consider, for example, human slavery. The early church accepted human slavery without reservation. Thus the author of the Ephesian letter could write:

> Slaves, be obedient to those who are your earthly masters, with fear and trembling, in singleness of heart, as to Christ; not in the way of eye service, as men-pleasers, but as servants of Christ, doing the will of God from the heart, rendering service with a good will as to the Lord and not to men, knowing that whatever good any one does, he will receive the same again from the Lord, whether he is a slave or free. (Eph 6:5–8)

In this passage being a slave is viewed as "doing the will of God." One of the letters in the New Testament is Paul's epistle to Philemon. This letter is a slavery document in which Paul advised Philemon, a slave owner, to be compassionate in dealing with a runaway slave named Onesimus. Similarly, when writing to the Colossian church he admonished slaves as follows:

85

Slaves, obey in everything those who are your earthly masters, not with eye service, as men-pleasers, but in singleness of heart, fearing the Lord. Whatever your task, work heartily, as serving the Lord and not men, knowing that from the Lord you will receive the inheritance as your reward; you are serving the Lord Christ. (Col 3:22–23)

In this statement Paul equates being a slave with "serving the Lord Christ." And the author of 1 Peter went so far as to advise slaves to obey abusive slave owners:

Slaves, be submissive to your masters with all respect, not only to the kind and gentle but also to the overbearing. For one is approved if, mindful of God, he endures pain while suffering unjustly. (1 Pet 2:18–19)

This statement in 1 Peter contains the curious suggestion that slaves should willingly endure pain while suffering unjustly. Back in the nineteenth century the clergy in the deep south appealed to passages like these to justify African slavery. They argued, "Early Christians believed in slavery. Jesus told parables involving slaves. Thus slavery is a legitimate institution. Indeed, it is the will of God." Nineteenth-century southern clergymen were right in contending the Bible is a pro-slavery document and that early Christians approved of slavery. Appealing to ethical intuition, however, other Christians concluded slavery was wrong and should be abolished. The early church's pro-slavery position has been rejected by much of contemporary society, and inquisitive Christians are under no obligation to accept the early church's pro-slavery stance.

Or consider the early church's negative attitude toward women. Paul wrote to the Corinthian church:

As in all the churches of the saints, the women should keep silence in the churches. For they are not permitted to speak, but should be subordinate, as even the law says. If there is anything they desire to know, let them ask their husbands at home. For it is shameful for a woman to speak in church.

(1 Cor 14:34–35)

For a woman to speak in church was a shameful deed. He also held the view that it was proper for a man not to touch a woman (1 Cor 7:1) and expressed the wish that all people were celibate like him (1 Cor 7:7). I know no reason why inquisitive Christians should adopt this Pauline negativity toward women. Yet on the basis of these Pauline statements many orthodox Christians approve of celibacy and an unmarried priesthood.

Another belief held by some in the early church, which inquisitive Christians today are not obligated to accept, is the view that Jesus' death by crucifixion was a sacrifice offered to God on behalf of sinful humanity. That some early Christians viewed Jesus' death as a sin sacrifice cannot be denied. The New Testament document that emphasizes this idea most prominently is the book of Hebrews.

But when Christ appeared as a high priest...he entered once for all into the Holy Place, taking not the blood of goats and calves but his own blood thus securing an eternal redemption. For if the sprinkling of defiled persons with the blood of goats and bulls and with the ashes of a heifer sanctifies for the purification of the flesh, how much more shall the blood of Christ, who through the eternal Spirit offered himself without blemish to God, purify your conscience from dead works to serve the living God. (Heb 9:11–14)

But as it is, he has appeared once for all at the end of the age to put away sin by the sacrifice of himself. And just as it is appointed for men to die once, and after that comes judgment, so Christ, having been offered once to bear the sins of many, will appear a second time, not to deal with sin but to save those who are eagerly waiting for him.

(Heb 9:26b–28)

In Hebrews, blood sacrifice and forgiveness are correlated. You can't have one without the other. Other New Testament documents express a similar view.

> If we walk in the light, as he is in the light, we have fellowship with one another, and the blood of Jesus his Son cleanses us from all sin. (1 John 1:7)

> You know that you were ransomed from the futile ways inherited from your fathers, not with perishable things such as silver or gold, but with the precious blood of Christ, like that of a lamb without blemish or spot. (1 Pet 1:19)

A similar thought is found in Rev 5:9 where Jesus is described as one who was slain and by means of his blood ransomed men for God.

That some early Christians viewed Jesus' crucifixion as a sin sacrifice is not surprising. Undoubtedly they were attempting to make sense out of Jesus' violent death. Moreover, sacrificing animals to appease and to please the gods was a common practice in Mediterranean and Near Eastern religions of two millennia ago. For example, an account appears in Acts of Paul and Barnabas visiting a city named Lystra. On this visit the people of Lystra mistook Barnabas for Zeus and they mistook Paul for Hermes. Whereupon "the priest of Zeus, whose temple was in front of the city, brought oxen and garlands to the gates and wanted to offer sacrifice with the people" (Acts 14:13). Animal sacrifice was practiced in Judaism and in the mystery religions like Mithraism with its taurobolium rite. In other words, sacrifice was a part of the religio-cultural air that early Christians breathed.

In the early Middle Ages, notably with theologians like St. Anselm, more and more emphasis was placed upon Jesus' execution as a sacrifice making possible divine forgiveness. Indeed, across the centuries the Christian faith has undergone what might be called a "cruxification process" — the centering of the Christian religion on the cross (in Latin *crux*). For some believers the cross is more important than the resurrection. For them, Jesus' sacrificial death is the Christian gospel. What was the main reason for Jesus appearing on this earth? The answer: to undergo a sacrificial death for mankind's sins. Noted church historian Jaroslav Pelikan has observed,

> The followers of Jesus concluded very early that he had lived in order to die, that his death was not the interruption of his life but its ultimate purpose. The creeds recognized this by moving directly from his birth "from the Virgin Mary" to his crucifixion "under Pontius Pilate." What was said of the thane of Cawdor in *Macbeth* was true preeminently of Jesus: "Nothing in his life became him like the leaving it." "Far be it from me," St. Paul said, "to glory except in the cross of our Lord Jesus Christ, by which the world has been crucified to me, and I to the world" (Gal 6:14).[1]

This emphasis upon Jesus' shed blood has become embedded in hymns sung Sunday after Sunday in church services. Once a belief has been embedded in a familiar hymn, it becomes unquestionable and sacrosanct. Ponder these words in a hymn by William Cowper:

> There is a fountain filled with *blood*
> drawn from Immanuel's veins;
> And sinners, plunged beneath that flood,
> lose all their guilty stains.

Or consider these words in a hymn by Robert Lowry:

> What can wash away my sin?
> Nothing but the *blood* of Jesus;
> What can make me whole again?
> Nothing but the *blood* of Jesus.

Probably the most familiar hymn in Protestantism is George Bennard's "The Old Rugged Cross." Millions of Christians have sung these words:

> On a hill far away stood an old rugged cross,
> The emblem of suffering and shame;
> And I love that old cross where the dearest and best
> For a world of lost sinners was slain.
> In the old rugged cross, stained with *blood* so divine,
> such a wonderful beauty I see;
> For 'twas on that old cross Jesus suffered and died,
> To pardon and sanctify me.

Churches emphasize the sacrificial death of Jesus when they observe holy communion. "The Order for the Administration of Holy Communion" in the United Methodist Church's *Book of Worship* contains sentences like these:

> Christ our Paschal Lamb is offered up for us, once for all, when he bore our sins on his body upon the cross; for he is the very Lamb of God that taketh away the sins of the world.

> Almighty God, our heavenly Father, who of thy tender mercy didst give thine only Son Jesus Christ to suffer death upon the cross for our redemption; who made there, by the one offering of himself, a full, perfect, and sufficient sacrifice for the sins of the whole world; and did institute, and in his holy gospel command us to continue, a perpetual memory of his precious death until his coming again: hear us, O merciful Father, we most humbly beseech thee.

Why the church sees fit to teach that Jesus' crucifixion was precious is not obvious. Be that as it may, the Methodist Church's view of holy communion (the Eucharist) is identical with that of Roman Catholicism in correlating blood and sacrifice with forgiveness of sins. The 1994 *Catechism of the Catholic Church* (page 344, section 1365) asserts, "In the Eucharist Christ gives us the very body which he gave up for us on the cross, the very blood which he 'poured out for many for the forgiveness of sins.'"

Theologians have spent untold hours hammering out atonement theories to explain why and how Jesus' death was sacrificial. This belief should be treated reverently and should never be ridiculed. For example, I do not think this belief should be referred to as "slaughterhouse" or "vampire" religion. I see no harm in people subscribing to this sacrificial view — a view held by many worthies of the church. When I was a youngster I held this view fervently. I shall never forget how my father "explained" to me one day what Jesus had accomplished on the cross. My father told me a story about a stolen lunch. Years ago students in the deep south carried their noon lunches to school in paper bags or in lunch boxes. When the noon lunch hour arrived it was discovered, so my father's story related, that one student's lunch had been stolen. Investigation revealed it had been stolen by a poor, frail youngster who had brought no lunch to school. He had stolen a lunch because he was hungry and had nothing to eat. The teacher decided to whip the youngster for theft. However, a muscular, healthy boy intervened and requested that he be whipped instead of the frail classmate. His request was granted. He was flogged in place of the thievish student. My father "explained" to me that this story illustrated what Jesus had done for me on the cross. He had taken the beating which I, a sinner, deserved. What I had to do in order to become a Christian was to believe Jesus had died for my sins and by so believing I would be "saved." I confess to the reader that I, at the time an elementary student in rural Mississippi, accepted my father's "substitutionary atonement theology" *without question.* I joined the church on the premise that Jesus had died for *my* sins. This was what the "gospel" was all about.

But there are questions that arise when attention is given to post-Enlightenment Jesus research. His sayings have been analyzed. This analysis makes clear that one is hard pressed to cite a single statement from the lips of the historical Jesus suggesting he viewed his death as a sin sacrifice. The only Jesus statement suggestive of this interpretation is Matt 26:28, which occurs in the context of the Last Supper. With reference to the wine cup Jesus said, "Drink of it, all of you; for this is my blood of the covenant, which is poured out for many for the forgiveness of sins." But this enigmatic statement presents problems. It does not appear in the Last Supper accounts found in the other gospels. Nor does it occur in our earliest record of the Last Supper (Paul's account in 1 Cor 11:23–26) wherein the bread and wine are viewed as tools for assisting memory. Does it make sense to construct atonement theories on a single problematic statement like Matt 26:28?

Moreover, Jesus made numerous statements about forgiveness in which there is no correlation between forgiveness and his crucifixion. Consider the forgiveness petition in the Lord's Prayer: "Forgive us our trespasses as we forgive those who trespass against us." Or consider the Jesus statement that immediately follows the Matthean version of the Lord's Prayer: "For if you forgive men their trespasses, your heavenly father will also forgive you; but if you do not forgive men their trespasses, neither will your father forgive your trespasses" (Matt 6:14–15). The thought content of these verses is similar to the thought content of the Jesus statement found in Luke: "Judge not, and you will not be judged; condemn not, and you will not be condemned; forgive, and you will be forgiven" (6:37). To the Capernaum paralytic (Matt 9:2–8, Mark 2:3–12, Luke 5:18–26) Jesus said, "My son, your sins are forgiven." While being crucified Jesus prayed, "Father, forgive them; for they know not what they do" (Luke 23:34). In none of these statements did Jesus correlate forgiveness and his crucifixion. Nor was the preaching of John the Baptist concerning forgiveness (Mark 1:4) so correlated. On one occasion Jesus was asked what a person must do to inherit eternal life (Matt 19:13–22). Jesus did not say, "Believe that my crucifixion is a sin sacrifice for you." Instead, Jesus replied, "If you would enter life, keep the commandments" (Matt 19:17). Thus Jesus taught that a blessed future life was dependent upon right moral behavior, not on personal acceptance of a blood sacrifice.

The problem is that the church's contention that Jesus' death was a sin sacrifice was fabricated with no attention given to what the historical Jesus thought and taught. A gap wider than the Grand Canyon exists between what Jesus believed and what orthodox Christianity says it believes. The church's gospel about Jesus is not the same as the gospel preached by Jesus. To express this matter another way, "The gospel or message preached by Jesus contains nothing of the later message preached concerning Jesus."[2] Or, as C. S. Lewis quipped, "The Gospel is not found in the gospels."

Nor did the church give attention to what Jesus actually experienced on a historical level in the closing hours of his life. Jesus' crucifixion is an example of bureaucratic brutality. He was executed by the Romans because they viewed him as a rebel against the empire. So understood Jesus' crucifixion has no religious significance. A historical understanding of Jesus' execution obviously does not harmonize with later attempts by the church to understand his execution as a religious event. If the major purpose for Jesus coming to this earth was to be crucified as a sin sacrifice, why did he pray to be delivered from that crucifixion (Matt 26:36–40)?

I find it ironic that on one Sunday a clergyman will condemn Pilate and the Roman soldiers for killing Jesus. "Pilate and the Roman soldiers were thugs! They should be ashamed of what they did!" But then on the next Sunday this same clergyman will explain that Jesus' death was a sin sacrifice carried out to fulfill God's will. If a clergyman believes Jesus' execution was the will of God, then should he not congratulate or applaud Pilate and the Roman soldiers for killing Jesus, thereby making possible redemption through his shed blood? Should not churches install altars to Pilate and the Roman soldiers where Christians can thank them for what they did? Or contrarily: Should Pilate and the Roman soldiers be viewed as unknowing puppets in God's hand? They thought they were executing a troublesome rebel; in reality they were slaughtering the Lamb of God who takes away the sins of the world. Poor fellows! They were ignorant pawns in God's scheme of salvation. Across the centuries they have been given a bad rap by the church.

The view that Jesus died on the cross as a sacrifice making possible forgiveness of sins is an entrenched Christian belief. Inquisitive Christians must realize there is no chance of this view being modified or abandoned by orthodox Christianity. Jesus' execution on a wooden cross outside Jerusalem has been romanticized. During Good Friday candy stores sell chocolate crosses, bakeries sell cross-shaped cakes coated with creamy icing, and Christians sing about loving the old rugged cross. Ireland's Waterford Crystal Limited produces crystal crosses for Easter and Christmas gifts, and women wear crosses around their necks for jewelry. Attempts by Christian thinkers to explain how the execution of a first-century rabbi accomplishes forgiveness for billions of people living centuries later are as perplexing as they are unconvincing. If it be true that familiarity breeds contempt, it is also true that familiarity blinds to grotesqueness. The view that God required a human sacrifice — Jesus' death — as something essential for divine forgiveness is as grotesque as it is repulsive. Curiously, theologians condemn human sacrifice in pagan religions while failing to perceive that they have placed the human sacrifice of Jesus at the core of Christendom's beliefs.

But reflective Christians are not obliged to believe Jesus' death was a sin sacrifice. They find this belief obnoxious. Instead, Jesus' execution should be categorized with Socrates' execution. Both were by-products of bureaucratic brutality and both poignantly exemplify man's inhumanity to man.

The view that Christians have their sins forgiven by believing in and accepting Jesus' sacrificial death (thereby being "saved" or "redeemed" or "born again") cuts the nerve for ethical enthusiasm. Why be concerned with the rightness or wrongness of personal behavior if Jesus' sacrifice cleanses the believer from his sins and, since he has been born again, gives him a free ride to heaven? The late William Alexander Percy, Mississippi delta aristocrat and planter from Greenville, Mississippi, wrote an autobiography entitled *Lanterns on the Levee: Recollections of a Planter's Son* in which he wrote,

> I asked a clergyman recently why it was that so many
> prominent churchgoers were crooks in business and

hypocrites in private life. He replied: "They have been born again." This clarified nothing for me and I told him as much. He explained sadly: "When they are born again, they are certain of salvation, and when you are certain of salvation you may do what you like." But I urged, horrified: "People don't really believe that!" "Hundreds of thousands of them," he rejoined, obviously as grieved as I. "The ethics of Jesus do not interest them when their rebirth guarantees them salvation."[3]

Notes

1. Jaroslav Pelikan, *The Illustrated Jesus through the Centuries* (New Haven: Yale University Press, 1997), 103. The following observation by Leslie D. Weatherhead is relevant:

It is obvious that, in every generation, men are at liberty to try to make sense of important events by reference to the thought-forms of their own time. The Jews were familiar with the age-long idea of obtaining a sense of forgiveness by sacrificing an animal on an altar. When therefore the early Christians, steeped in Judaism, were confronted with the execution of Jesus, it is no wonder that, to make sense of it, to explain an omnipotent God's non-interference and Christ's willingness to die (since he could easily have escaped), their minds hit on the idea of sacrifice, and Jesus, whom John the Baptist had called the Lamb of God, was thought to be the climax of the age-long sacrifices in the temple, and it is probable that Paul thought in this way also. Paul was a great theologian as well as a great saint and a heroic missionary, but we are not bound to imprison our minds in his theories. Newton was a great scientist, but it is no disparagement of Newton to realize that even schoolboys today know more than he did about atoms. Thought moves on in every field of inquiry. (From Weatherhead, *The Christian Agnostic* [Nashville: Abingdon, 1965], 116–17)

Also relevant is Paula Fredriksen's observation that animal sacrifice was a very prominent feature of worship in antiquity. She describes animal sacrifice as "the single biggest difference between the religious sensibility of people in the modern West and our cultural ancestors of twenty centuries ago.... Universally, the worship of a deity — virtually any deity — involved the slaughter of animals.... Purificatory rites helped prepare the worshiper for his or her encounter, through sacrifice, with the sacred." See pages 51–52 of Paula Fredriksen's *Jesus of Nazareth, King of the Jews* (New York: Vintage Books, 1999).

2. Von Harnack's distinction between the gospel preached *by Jesus* and the early church's gospel *about Jesus* (the messenger supplants the message) was explained by the late Paul Tillich as follows: "There is another side to Harnack which was much more impressive for the masses of educated people at the turn of the century. He himself once told me that in the year 1900 the main railway station in the city of Leipzig, one of the largest in Central Europe, was blocked by freight cars in which his book *What Is Christianity?* was being sent all over the world. He also told us that this book was being translated into more languages than any other book except the Bible. This means that this book, which was the religious witness of one of the greatest scholars of the century, had great significance to the educated people prior to the First World War. It meant the possibility of affirming the Christian message in a form which was free from its dogmatic captivity and at the same time very much rooted in the biblical image of Jesus. But in order to elaborate this image, he invented the formula *that distinguished sharply between the gospel of Jesus and the gospel about Jesus.* He stated that the gospel about Jesus does not belong in the gospel preached by Jesus. This is the classical formula of liberal theology: the gospel or message preached by Jesus contains nothing of the later message preached concerning Jesus." Paul Tillich, *A History of Christian Thought from Its Judaic and Hellenistic Origins to Existentialism* (ed. Carl E. Braaten; New York: Simon & Schuster, 1967), 518–19.

3. William Alexander Percy, *Lanterns on the Levee: Recollections of a Planter's Son* (New York: Knopf, 1959), 314.

Chapter 10

Strategy Three

*Beware of the Tendency to Sentimentalize Jesus
and the Tendency to Aggrandize Jesus*

Inquisitive believers can rescue Jesus from the Christians by distinguishing the pre-resurrection Jesus from the post-resurrection Jesus and by realizing they are not obligated to believe everything early Christians believed. Inquisitive Christians should beware of two distorting, and contradictory, tendencies existing within Christianity: (1) the tendency to sentimentalize Jesus and (2) the tendency to aggrandize Jesus. These contradictory tendencies make it impossible for us to have a realistic, meaningful understanding of either the pre- or post-resurrection Jesus.

By sentimentalization I am referring to the tendency of some Christians to view Jesus in an overly personal or maudlin or sugary manner. This sentimentalizing proclivity is exhibited in automobile bumper stickers that read "Jesus is my buddy" and T-shirts that declare "Jesus is a pal." We encounter this sentimentalizing tendency in religious art. Perhaps the most recognized sentimental portrait of Jesus is Warner Sallman's *Head of Christ,* and Sallman's associated paintings, such as *Christ at Heart's Door, The Lord is My Shepherd,* and *He Careth for You.* These pictures have been described accurately as Protestant icons, for they adorn Sunday school classrooms and sanctuaries and provide the image of Jesus with which most Protestant Christians identify. Sallman's art portrays Jesus as "everyone's friend."[1]

Evangelical Christianity in particular abounds with hymns that suggest a sentimental intimacy with Jesus. These hymns also tend to be egocentric; they are filled with personal pronouns like I and me. One of the first hymns some youngsters learn to sing is the Anna Warner hymn entitled "Jesus Loves Me."

Jesus loves me! this I know, for the Bible tells me so;
Little ones to him belong; they are weak, but he is strong.

Jesus loves me! loves me still, Tho' I'm very weak and ill;
From his shining throne on high, comes to watch me
    where I lie.

Jesus loves me! He will stay close beside me all the way;
If I love him, when I die He will take me home on high.

Yes, Jesus loves me. Yes, Jesus loves me,
Yes, Jesus loves me, the Bible tells me so.

Sunday after Sunday congregations sing the Lela Long hymn entitled "Jesus is the Sweetest Name I Know." In this hymn the name of Jesus is identified with sweetness.

Jesus is the sweetest name I know,
 and he's just the same as His lovely name,
And that's the reason why I love him so;
Oh, Jesus is the sweetest name I know.

Lela Long's hymn reduces Christian discipleship to a love affair with Jesus. A similar thought is found in the Frederick Whitfield hymn entitled "Oh, How I Love Jesus."

There is a name I love to hear, I love to sing its worth;
It sounds as music in my ear, the sweetest name on earth.
Oh, how I love Jesus, Oh how I love Jesus,
Oh, how I love Jesus, because he first loved me.

Christians sing about Jesus being their friend. Consider the Joseph Scriven hymn entitled "What a Friend We have in Jesus." Or ponder the words of the Jeremiah Rankin hymn entitled "Tell It to Jesus."

Are you weary, are you heavy hearted?
Tell it to Jesus, tell it to Jesus;

Are you grieving over joys departed?
Tell it to Jesus alone.
Tell it to Jesus, tell it to Jesus,
He is a friend that's well known;
You've no other such a friend or brother,
Tell it to Jesus alone.

Other hymns such as "My Jesus, I Love Thee," "Jesus Is All the World to Me," "I've Found a Friend, O Such a Friend," "Walking Along with Jesus," and "In the Garden" send a similar message. In this last hymn we are informed that Jesus' voice is so sweet that the "birds hush their singing." This hymn also informs us that Jesus walks with us and talks with us.

In all of these popular hymns Jesus is conceived as a sweet, heavenly concierge who loves and helps Christians. Across the years this sweetening-of-Jesus process has puzzled me. Where, when, and why did this sugaring process begin? Other religions do not have this sugary portrayal of the heroes of their faith. I have never heard a Jew sing, "Oh, how I love Abraham" or "Oh, how I love Moses." I have never heard a Jew sing, "Moses is the sweetest name I know." Nor have I heard a Buddhist sing, "Siddhartha Gautama is the sweetest name I know." Nor have I heard a Zoroastrian sing, "Zarathustra is the sweetest name I know." Reflective reading of the New Testament gospels suggests Jesus was not a "sweet" person (nor was Moses or Muhammad). A "sweet" Jesus would not have antagonized the Jewish religious leaders of his day. Nor would a "sweet" Jesus advocating intimate friendship have incurred the wrath of the Roman authorities.

Could it be that viewing Jesus as one who loves and helps us is nothing more than an exercise in autosuggestion — the subconscious adoption of an idea originating within oneself? Assuming Jesus is God, as orthodox Christianity contends, would it not be comforting to believe Jesus is our friend and helper with whom, in troubling times, we can have an intimate relationship? Someone once asked Albert Einstein, "What is the most significant question a person can ask?" Einstein answered, "Is the universe friendly?" The destructive forces of hurricanes and disease and the debilitating effects of violent crime (natural and moral evil) suggest the universe is not always friendly. Wouldn't it be comforting to believe that in this at-times indifferent and unfriendly universe we have a friend and helper in Jesus, the Son of God?

Be that as it may, in some places the Christian faith has been transformed into a self-serving Jesus cult. Jesusolatry, the worship of Jesus, has supplanted the worship of God the creator and sustainer of life. It is possible for Jesus cultists to oversell Jesus by presenting him as a genie who exists to do the will of those who call upon him as his disciples.

Just as much as the church tends to sentimentalize Jesus, it also tends to aggrandize him. By "aggrandizing" I mean the tendency to enhance someone's reputation and to make someone appear greater than the evidence allows. Christians have so aggrandized Jesus, emphasizing his divinity at the expense of his humanity, that he has become a figure remote from ordinary human experience. He now resides in speculative dogmas and in stained-glass windows.

Jude is an obscure letter, the next-to-last document in the New Testament. It contains the puzzling belief that the archangel Michael and the devil disputed over the corpse of Moses (Jude 9). This letter by Jude begins, "I found it necessary to write appealing to you to contend for the faith which was once for all delivered to the saints." This phrase seems to suggest that the Christian faith is a static belief system, comparable to a treasure of rubies and diamonds, which appeared on the world scene some two thousand years ago. Moreover, Christians should pass on this crystallized faith from one generation to the next. Many Christians believe that what the church teaches today is what the church has always taught. "The church has always believed in the incarnation." "The church has always believed in the blessed Trinity." "The church has always believed in the inspiration of the Bible." "The church has always believed in the seven sacraments."

Post-Enlightenment scholarship has made it clear, however, that Christian beliefs, rather than being static, have been dynamic. Across the centuries various beliefs have surged and then subsided. Nowhere has the fluidity of Christian beliefs been more obvious than beliefs attempting to answer the questions: Who was Jesus of Nazareth and who is Jesus? In the church's vocabulary the term Christology, the "study of Christ," reflects upon the person and work of Jesus Christ.

The New Testament makes it clear that from the outset Christians pondered the question: Who is Jesus? What are we to make of him? No single answer was given to this question. Indeed, even a casual reading of the New Testament reveals that the early church applied to Jesus a plethora of names and titles. They referred to him as the prophet from Nazareth, Son of God, Son of Man, Messiah or Christ, lord, son of David, lamb of God, Immanuel, savior, the Logos or Word, and a priest after the order of Melchizedek (Heb 5:6). The variety of these terms suggests that early Christian thinkers were befuddled as to Jesus' identity. They knew he was a significant person, but they had little better idea about how to express that significance than we. Over the years hundreds of books and journal articles have been written seeking to explain the meaning of the various titles that have been ascribed to Jesus. Frequently these books and journal articles commit what can be called the "naming fallacy," which assumes that because a phenomenon has been given a name it has been explained. I teach at a state university. My colleagues in the physics department tell me no one has ever explained why objects thrown into the air fall back to earth. Throw a ball into the air and back to earth it comes. Obviously there is a force that causes the ball to fall back to earth, and this attracting force has been given the name of gravity. But giving this attracting force the name of gravity does not explain what that force is or why it functions as it does. Gravity remains a scientific puzzle. Similarly, theologians — capitulating to the "naming fallacy" — think that by ascribing names to Jesus — like Messiah or Son of God — and expounding what those terms mean they have thereby explained Jesus. They fail to realize that Jesus eludes precise analysis or explanation. As Huston Smith says, "We will never understand who Jesus was or what God accomplished through him."[2]

The earliest Christian literature that has come down to us makes no attempts to grasp in detail Jesus' inner being or essence. But as the years rolled by Christian thinkers began trying to do this. Christian theology became increasingly speculative. Out of speculative attempts to analyze Jesus' inner being arose what has come to be known as the doctrine of the incarnation and the doctrine of the trinity. Thus curiously the Christian religion, which began as an eschatological movement ("The kingdom of God is about to come!" and "Jesus will soon return on the clouds of glory!"), mutated into a belief system concerning Jesus' identity and mission.

The incarnation and trinity doctrines, both dealing with Jesus' inner being, did not crystallize officially until the fourth century of the Christian era. The earliest adherents of the Christian movement did not have time to ponder philosophically Jesus' inner being. They faced daily the possibility of being executed by Roman authorities who viewed them as participating in a seditious religion. Absorbed with life and death matters, they had scant time for theological-philosophical reflection.

By the fourth century c.e., however, the situation changed. Constantine became the Roman Empire's ruler and is remembered as its first Christian emperor. He issued an edict of toleration that ended state persecution of Christians. Moreover, he established Christianity as the official state religion.

This changed situation provided Christians time and opportunity for reflection. Toward that end church councils met during the fourth and fifth centuries to decide how best to present Christianity to the world at large. Bishops attending these councils employed philosophical language. Their reflections were summarized in creeds, which in turn were used as measuring rods of orthodoxy. If believers could repeat the words of these creeds, they were considered orthodox. If they could not conscientiously repeat these creeds, they were considered heretics and were often punished for their disbelief.

Out of these early church councils came the incarnation and trinity doctrines. Their formulation was a by-product of what church historians refer to as the Arian controversy. This controversy takes its name from an old-timer named Arius. Arius, a respected man of learning and piety, was a church official in an Egyptian city named Baucalis. Trained theologically in Antioch of Syria, he emphasized in his thinking the unity of God. He taught that Christ was a created being and was not of the substance of God. He also taught that Jesus — like other creatures — was made out of "nothing" and was not eternal. "The Son has a beginning . . . but God is without beginning." This type of theologizing and speculation strikes us today as being unwarranted, quaint, and obscure. But it did not seem unwarranted, quaint, or obscure to a contemporary of Arius named Alexander, Arius's bishop in Alexandria in Egypt. As far as Alexander was concerned, Jesus was eternal, was identical in essence with God the Father, and was uncreated. This disagreement between Arius and Alexander threw the ecclesiastical world of the Roman Empire into turmoil — much to the consternation of Constantine, who viewed the disagreement as "an unprofitable question." To settle the controversy he convened what has become known as the First General Council of the church. Some three hundred bishops gathered (at government expense) in May of 325 C.E. at Nicaea, a city in Asia Minor (now Turkey) close to Constantinople, which had recently become the new capital of the Roman Empire. Constantine was present at this council. As emperor, the most powerful man of that day, he addressed the assembled bishops and exhorted them to maintain "harmony and peace" within the church. In other words, enough of this Arian controversy! The bishops put their heads together and out of this church council came what is known as the Nicene Creed. This creed reads as follows:

We believe in one God the Father All-sovereign, maker of all things visible and invisible;

And in one Lord Jesus Christ, the Son of God, *begotten of the Father*, only-begotten, *that is, of the substance of the Father*, God of God, Light of Light, *true God of true God, begotten not made, of one substance with the Father*, through whom all things were made, *things in heaven and things on the earth;* who for us men and for our salvation *came down* and was made flesh, *and became man*, suffered, and rose on the third day, ascended into the heavens, is coming to judge living and dead.

And in the Holy Spirit.

And those that say "There was when he was not," and, "Before he was begotten he was not," and that, "He came into being from what-is-not," or those that allege, that the Son of God is "Of another substance or essence" or "created," or "changeable" or "alterable," these the Catholic and Apostolic church anathematizes.

Ponder the words of this creed.[3] Jesus is described as being "God of God" and "true God of true God." The creed further asserts that Jesus is of the *substance* of the Father. The non-biblical word translated as *substance* is the Greek word *ousia*, which means substance or stuff or essence. This assertion is what is meant by the doctrine of the incarnation: the uniting of deity with humanity in Jesus Christ. For the creed affirms that Jesus who was "true God of true God" for us men and for our salvation "came down" and "became man." This Nicene view that Jesus was made of godly substance (*ousia*) is what I mean by the aggrandizing — the elevating — of Jesus to divine status. "Jesus equals God." Unfortunately, none of the bishops at Nicaea had read Immanuel Kant. Thus they were unaware of human finitude. That no one can "know" the substance (*ousia*) of either God or Jesus never crossed their minds. Nevertheless, across the centuries the church has viewed the Nicene Creed — with its insistence on the incarnation and with its trinity formula (We believe in one God the Father...and in one Lord Jesus Christ...and in the Holy Spirit) — as being *the* authoritative statement of what Christians believe about God and Jesus.

In the wake of the Nicene Council, Arius was banished into exile at the command of Constantine. Constantine ordered that Arius's writings be burned. Arius's supporters were also sent into exile. Thus the unity of the church was achieved through imperial intervention.

A hidden agenda was operative at the Council of Nicaea. That hidden agenda had to do with the Greek Orthodox conception of salvation. Christians in the Greek-speaking eastern Mediterranean world believed in what is called *theosis:* transforming the human into the divine or the transformation of sinful mortality into divine and blessed immortality. They believed the Christian faith enabled a believer to become divine. Only by God coming into union with humanity in Christ could the transformation of the human into the divine be accomplished or be mediated by Christ to his disciples. As Athanasius, the successor to Alexander as bishop of Alexandria and the defender par excellence of Nicene orthodoxy, expressed the matter: "He (Christ) was made man that we might be made divine." To this way of thinking Arianism provided no basis for salvation.

But what must be understood is that this Greek Orthodox conception of salvation (*theosis*)[4] and the doctrines of the incarnation and trinity were fashioned by the church of the fourth century with no attention to the historical Jesus. I know of no statement made by the synoptic Jesus suggesting his disciples were to become divine. Instead, they were to enjoy eating bread and drinking wine in the kingdom of God. Nor do I know of any statement made by the synoptic Jesus suggesting he believed he was God. Nevertheless, the *theosis* conception of salvation still prevails in the Eastern Orthodox Church and the doctrines of the incarnation and trinity prevail today in Eastern Orthodoxy, Roman Catholicism, and Protestantism.

After the Council of Nicaea christological reflection within the church became even more doctrinaire or speculative. Christian thinkers began debating the question: How was Jesus' human nature related to his divine nature? Which dimension was dominant: the divine or the human? This debate over the human and the divine in Jesus was "settled" in 451 c.e. at the Fourth Ecumenical Council. This council met at Chalcedon, a city immediately across the Bosporus from Constantinople. Some six hundred bishops attended the conference. They adopted what in the history of Christian doctrine is called the Creed of Chalcedon. This creed contends Jesus was completely and simultaneously both God and man. The heart of the creed reads as follows:

> Following the holy fathers we all, with one voice, define that there is to be confessed one and the same Son, our Lord Jesus Christ, perfect in Godhead and perfect in manhood, truly god and truly man, of rational soul and body, of the same substance with the Father according to the Godhead, and of the same substance with us according to the manhood, like to us in all respects, without sin, begotten of the Father before all time according to the Godhead, in these latter days, for us and for our salvation, born of the Virgin Mary, the Mother of God according to the manhood, one and the same Christ, Son, Lord, Only-begotten, in two natures, inconfusedly, immutably, indivisibly, inseparately, the distinction of natures being by no means taken away by the union, but rather the peculiarity of each nature being preserved and concurring in one person and one substance not parted or separated into two persons, but one and the same Son and Only-begotten, divine word the Lord Jesus Christ; as from the beginning the prophets declared concerning him, and the Lord Jesus Christ has taught us, and the creed of the holy fathers has transmitted to us.

On an earlier page I stated that I saw no harm in Christians believing Jesus' death was a sacrifice for sins. Similarly, I see no harm in Christians believing in the blessed Trinity, in the Nicene view of the incarnation, and in Chalcedonian Christology. These beliefs are entrenched in orthodox Christianity, will never be modified or abandoned, are held in esteem by millions of Christians, and should never be ridiculed. For example, I do not believe the Trinity doctrine should be referred to as "three gods in a pod." But a coterie of reflective Christians find these doctrines hard to swallow. They view them as an excess of affirmation. They are aware these doctrines cannot be harmonized with the teachings of the synoptic Jesus uncovered by post-Enlightenment scholarship. Additionally, these doctrines so etherealize Jesus that he becomes irrelevant to everyday human life. "How can a sinless God in human flesh — one of the Trinity — understand what it is like to be a cotton farmer in Alabama or a diner waitress in Chicago?" Moreover, thinking Christians suspect that the hundreds of bishops gathered at Nicaea in the fourth century and at Chalcedon in the fifth century are comparable to Ludwig II of Bavaria, the dream king. Ludwig built across Bavaria magnificent castles — like Neuschwanstein and Linderhof — which still impress people as far as their ornate beauty is concerned. But Ludwig spent and built beyond his financial means. He ended up in bankruptcy. Similarly, have not theologians in the past speculated beyond their mental means? They have sought to diagram God and to grasp intellectually Jesus' inner being. This we cannot do. God remains *deus absconditus* (the hidden God). Isaiah recognized this when he said: "Truly, you are a God who hides himself, O God of Israel, the Savior" (45:15). Likewise, Jesus' precise identity remains unknowable. There are limitations to what we can understand. A person who holds the view that God is hidden is not an atheist. On the contrary, he is a theist. And the person who holds the view that Jesus' precise identity is unknowable is not a skeptic. To the contrary, he accepts Jesus' historical facticity.[5]

Thus the church has aggrandized Jesus with extravagant doctrinal and dogmatic claims that reflective Christians find difficult to accept and difficult to keep on repeating. This aggrandizing process, not surprisingly, was present from the very beginning of the Christian movement and is evident in the gospels in the New Testament. For example, at Jesus' birth a host of angels appeared in the sky (Luke 2:13–14) and sang, "Glory to God in the highest." During Jesus' baptism the heavens opened and a voice thundered, "This is my beloved Son, with whom I am well pleased" (Matt 3:17). How the heavens can be opened is not clear. On one occasion Jesus took Peter and James to a high mountain (Matt 17:1–8). On this mountain he was transfigured before them, his face shone like the sun, and his clothes became white as light. Moses and Elijah mysteriously appeared, a bright cloud overshadowed them, and a voice from the cloud affirmed, "This is my beloved Son." At the time of the crucifixion an earthquake occurred (Matt 27:51) and darkness fell over all the land (Matt 27:45). The curtain in the temple was torn in two from top to bottom; the tombs were opened and saints who had fallen asleep were raised from the dead, went into Jerusalem, and appeared to many (Matt 27:51–52). All of these are nonhistorical, aggrandizing embellishments.

Students of the New Testament have always been perplexed by a category of miracles, in which Jesus exercises control over nature such as walking on the water of the Sea of Galilee, labeled the "nature miracles." Scholars ponder the question: What is the purpose of the "nature miracles"? Could some of them be viewed as pious attempts by the early church to aggrandize Jesus? Consider the Nature Miracle referred to as the "stilling of the storm."

> On that day, when evening had come, he said to them, "Let us go across to the other side." And leaving the crowd, they took him with them, just as he was, in the boat. And other boats were with him. And a great storm of wind arose, and the waves beat into the boat, so that the boat was already filling. But he was in the stern, asleep on the cushion; and they woke him and said to him, "Teacher, do you not care if we perish?" And he awoke and rebuked the wind, and said to the sea, "Peace! Be still!" And the wind ceased, and there was a great calm. He said to them, "Why are you afraid? Have you no faith?" And they were filled with awe,

and said to one another, "Who then is this, that even wind and sea obey him?" (Mark 4:35–41)

This account relates that Jesus spoke to and calmed the wind. A similar episode occurs in Book I of Virgil's *Aeneid,* the national epic of ancient Rome written in the last half of the first century C.E. Neptune, the sea god, saw the fleet of Aeneas being battered and threatened in a sea storm. He summoned the East and West winds and rebuked them: "Does family pride tempt you to such impertinence? Do you really dare, you Winds, without my divine assent to confound the earth and sky, and raise this riot of water?" Before Neptune stopped speaking "the insurgent sea was calmed, the mob of cloud dispersed, and the sun restored to power."[6] Both in Mark's and Virgil's stories a sea storm occurs, a hero addresses the wind, the wind obeys the hero's voice, and calm is restored to the sea. A conjecture: Could the stilling-of-the-storm episode in the Gospels be an aggrandizing story to show that Jesus was as powerful as Neptune?

Or consider the puzzling account of Jesus walking on the water of the Sea of Galilee.

Then he made the disciples get into the boat and go before him to the other side, while he dismissed the crowds. And after he had dismissed the crowds, he went up into the hills by himself to pray. When evening came, he was there alone, but the boat by this time was many furlongs distant from the land, beaten by the waves; for the wind was against them.

And in the fourth watch of the night he came to them, walking on the sea. But when the disciples saw him walking on the sea, they were terrified, saying, "It is a ghost!" And they cried out for fear. But immediately he spoke to them, saying, "Take heart, it is I; have no fear." (Matt 14:22–27)

Life-of-Jesus scholars have wrestled with the question: What was the point or purpose of Jesus walking on water? Again maybe the answer to this query is to be found in the *Aeneid.*

In Book I, line 147 Neptune is described by Virgil as one who rides in his chariot "over the face of the waters." Could the walking-on-the-water episode in the Gospels be an aggrandizing story to show that Jesus like Neptune could transport himself over water?

This line of reasoning would appeal to potential converts to Christianity living in the Roman Empire. Maybe John Macquarrie is right in doubting "whether any nature miracles were ever performed by Jesus."[7] Or maybe John Dominic Crossan is right in contending that the nature miracles are parables. He advances this view in his autobiography entitled *A Long Way from Tipperary.*

But Christians should not be surprised or vexed by the presence in the Gospels of aggrandizing embellishments. Ancient literature abounded with aggrandizing, embellishing details and this literature was not viewed as being fraudulent. We must remember that modern historiography (attempts to tell about the past as it actually happened without frills and bells) did not begin to flourish until the nineteenth century. Every student of the Gospels should read Suetonius's *The Lives of the Twelve Caesars,* an account of the rulers of the Roman Empire from Julius Caesar through Domitian. Suetonius was secretary to the Roman emperor Hadrian. He wrote of events that took place at the very time the Christian religion was emerging on the world scene and the Gospels were being written. Concerning the death of Julius Caesar, Suetonius wrote: "He died in the fifty-sixth year of his age, and was numbered among the gods, not only by a formal decree, but also in the conviction of the vulgar. For at the first of the games which his heir Augustus gave in honor of his apotheosis, a comet shone for seven successive days, rising about the eleventh hour, and was believed to be the soul of Caesar, who had been taken to heaven."[8] Or concerning the night during which a woman named Atia conceived Caesar Augustus, founder of the empire, Suetonius wrote that she was impregnated by a serpent while she slept in the temple of Apollo.

I doubt if any reader of Suetonius today believes that for seven successive days a comet appeared over Rome just before sunset and was the departed soul of Julius Caesar. Likewise, I doubt if any Suetonius reader today believes Caesar Augustus's mother was impregnated one night by a serpent in the temple of Apollo.

Yet ancient literature abounds with such embellishments. These fanciful particulars were literary devices employed by authors to make their accounts interesting. Josephus, a first-century Jewish historian, wrote that during the siege of Jerusalem by the Romans, a star appeared shaped like a sword, a heifer gave birth to a lamb in the Jewish temple, at sunset chariots and troops of soldiers ran about in the clouds, and one night a great light shone so brightly around the temple altar that it appeared to be day time (*Jewish War,* VI.5). Livy, a Roman historian who was a contemporary of Augustus, recounted that during Fabius's third consulship the sea caught on fire, a cow gave birth to a colt, Lanuvium statues in the temple of Juno Sospita oozed blood, and stones rained from the sky (*History of Rome,* XXIII.31).

Relying on intuition, we take these Suetonius, Josephus, and Livy reports with a grain of salt. Similarly, I think Christians can take with a grain of salt the report that an angelic choir sang in the sky the night Jesus was born or the report that at Jesus' baptism the heavens opened (an astronomical impossibility) and a voice announced from heaven that Jesus was God's son. While a seminarian I heard a theology professor from Germany say, "The trouble with you Americans is that you want to take everything literally." The professor was right.[9]

Thinking Christians can rescue Jesus from orthodox Christianity by not capitulating to two contrary tendencies: the tendency to sentimentalize Jesus and the tendency to aggrandize him. Whatever else he was, Jesus was no "sweet" person. He was an opinionated, at-times-abrasive, headstrong rabbi. Attempts to transform him into a "sugary" person produces a debased version of the Christian faith that has little relevance to the problems of evil and human suffering. A sentimentalized Jesus may be appropriate for children but not for adults living in an often sad and sordid world.

On the other hand, thinking Christians, by being aware of the aggrandizing tendency, can be delivered from the tyranny of dogma. One is not compelled to believe in Chalcedonian Christology or the Trinity in order to be a Christian. Unfortunately, across the centuries some Christians have believed you must accept these doctrines. They have also believed they were placed on earth to impose these doctrines on others. For example, the Crusaders illustrate the horrific zeal with which Christians sought to convert non-Christians to their particular way of believing. The church also burned many people at the stake who did not agree with what had come to be accepted as authoritative church doctrine. The church called people who did not agree with official church doctrine heretics. Perhaps one of the most horrible examples of the persecution of a heretic is the death of Servetus. He was tortured and then burned at the stake for his belief that the doctrine of the trinity was an error.

Notes

1. David Morgan, "The Likeness of Christ in Sallman's Art" in *Icons of American Protestantism: The Art of Warner Sallman* (ed. David Morgan; New Haven: Yale University Press, 1996), 192. This book is a study of the visual piety of mid-twentieth-century conservative American Protestantism. The photographic reproductions are superb.

2. Huston Smith, "Jesus and the World's Religions" in *Jesus at 2000* (ed. Marcus Borg; Boulder, Colo.: Westview Press, 1998), 113.

3. Henry Bettenson, ed., *Documents of the Christian Church* (London: Oxford University Press, 1947), 36. In the creed Jesus is described as "true God of true God." This way of thinking about Jesus ("Jesus is God") is not in harmony with the main drift of early Christian thought. There are, it must be acknowledged, a few statements in the New Testament that refer to Jesus as God. They can be numbered on the fingers of one hand; none of them are Jesus statements. In John 20:28 Thomas refers to Jesus as "my lord and my God." The prologue to the Fourth Gospel contains the assertion (John 1:1) that "the Word was God." Matt 1:23 refers the term "Immanuel" (which means "God with us") to Jesus, and in Heb 1:8 a psalm is addressed to Jesus as God ("Thy throne, O God, is for ever . . ."). Otherwise, the New Testament writers were hesitant to refer to Jesus as God.

4. A hint of *theosis* is found in 2 Pet 1:3–4. With reference to God the epistle asserts: "His divine power has granted to us all things that pertain to life and godliness, through the knowledge of him who called us to his own glory and

excellence, by which he has granted to us his precious and very great promises, that through these you may escape from the corruption that is in the world, and become partakers of the divine nature."

5. With church historian Jaroslav Pelikan, that person might say, "Regardless of what anyone may personally think or believe about him, Jesus of Nazareth has been the dominant figure in the history of Western culture for almost twenty centuries. If it were possible, with some sort of super magnet, to pull out of that history every scrap of metal bearing at least a trace of his name, how much would be left? It is from his birth that most of the human race dates its calendars, by his name that millions curse, and in his name that millions pray" (*The Illustrated Jesus through the Centuries* [New Haven: Yale University Press, 1997], 114). The person who accepts Jesus' historical facticity might also agree with historian Kenneth Scott Latourette's remark that "Jesus Christ has been the most influential life lived on this planet," as stated in his *A History of Christianity* (New York: Harper and Brothers, 1953), 1476.

6. Virgil, *The Aeneid* (trans. Cecil Day Lewis; London: Oxford University Press, 1952), 14.

7. John Macquarrie, *Jesus Christ in Modern Thought* (Philadelphia: Trinity Press International, 1990), 38.

8. Suetonius, *The Lives of the Twelve Caesars* (ed. Joseph Gavorse; New York: Modern Library, 1931), 49–50.

9. Hellenistic literature is also full of miraculous births, miracle workers, and resurrections from the dead. For primary sources, see David L. Dungan and David R. Cartlidge, *Documents for the Study of the Gospels* (Philadelphia: Fortress Press, 1980). For an account of the ways that these Hellenistic stories influenced the stories of Jesus, see Gregory J. Riley, *One Jesus, Many Christs: How Jesus Inspired Not One True Christianity, but Many: The Truth About Christian Origins* (San Francisco: HarperSanFrancisco, 1997), and Dennis R. MacDonald, ed., *Mimesis and Intertextuality in Antiquity and Christianity* (Harrisburg, Pa.: Trinity Press International, 2001).

Chapter 11

Strategy Four

Rejoice in Religious Pluralism

Inquisitive believers can also rescue Jesus from orthodox Christianity by accepting and rejoicing in religious pluralism. "Religious pluralism" refers to the undeniable fact that we live in a world in which many religions coexist. Christianity is not the only faith. Religions such as Judaism, Islam, Buddhism, Hinduism, and Shinto are also a part of the world scene. The reality of religious pluralism has been brought home to me in a personal way as a result of teaching for over three decades at a state university. Over the years I have taught Jewish, Buddhist, Shinto, and Hindu students. I have intuited depths of piety — a reverence for God — in these non-Christian students. Their religion is meaningful to them. They would never consider "converting" to Christianity.

The existence of these non-Christian religions poses a problem for Christians conditioned to believe their faith is the only valid religion. "We Christians have a monopoly on religious truth and other religions are false." Functioning on this presupposition, churches expend energy and invest vast sums of money on "foreign mission" enterprises to convert people of other faiths to Christianity. They justify "foreign missions" by appealing to a statement allegedly made by Jesus: "I am the way, and the truth, and the life; no one comes to the Father but by me" (John 14:6). In John's Gospel, Jesus speaks repeatedly and primarily about himself. He makes such egocentric claims as "I am the door" and "I am the true vine" and "I am the good shepherd" and "I am the bread of life" and "I am the light of the world." In keeping with this motif the Jesus of the Fourth Gospel claims, "I am the way, and the truth, and the life; no one comes to the Father but by me." Evangelical Christians use this statement as a basis for their view that Christianity is the only valid religion. But did Jesus utter this exclusivist claim or was this claim placed on Jesus' lips by the unknown author of the Fourth Gospel? Contemporary scholarship contends that these words were put in Jesus' mouth by the unknown author of the Fourth Gospel, not uttered by Jesus himself. We are under no obligation to accept his view as valid.

We must bear in mind that the biblical world is the Near East and Mediterranean lands. The Bible displays no knowledge of the Far East. No evidence exists suggesting early Jewish and Christian thinkers, including Jesus, were aware of religions like Hinduism and Buddhism, though they existed long before Christianity and were contemporaries of Judaism. But religions like these continue to manifest a resolute vitality. They have not faded away and no prospect exists of them fading away. Church historian Roland Bainton observes

> Despite the impressiveness of the geographical spread of Christianity, it cannot be said that the world has been won for Christ in our generation. No serious dent has been made on the other major religions of the world — Judaism, Islam, Hinduism, Buddhism, and Confucianism. The great gains have been at the expense of primitive religions, notably animism. In lands where there has been prodigious missionary endeavor the percentage of Christians remains small. It is estimated that before the Second World War the Christians in India numbered two percent of the total population; in China it was only one percent, and in Japan a mere one-half percent. Christianity is a minority religion in the world at large, as it always has been.[1]

Thus Christians face a dilemma: What are they to make of the minority status of Christianity and the vitality of non-Christian religions? A major reaction over the years has been to give a religion like Buddhism the thumbs-down treatment. Orthodox Christianity still operates according to the belief that it is the exclusive path to God. Although other religions might have their own practices and beliefs, these religions are really just pathways to the one true religion, Christianity. Thus, it is not unusual for orthodox Christians to condemn other religious beliefs because they are not on the right path to God.

Reflective Christians find such beliefs disconcerting. But such beliefs are not obligatory for Christians. Thinking Christians can rescue Jesus from such savage beliefs by rejoicing in, rather than resenting, religious pluralism. They can agree with a statement made by Simon Peter in the context of his visit to the Gentile home of Cornelius at Caesarea: "Truly I perceive that God shows no partiality, but in every nation any one who fears him and does what is right is acceptable to him" (Acts 10:34–35).

A case can be made for the view that Christianity has arrived at a "hinge moment" or a "turning point" in its history. Instead of viewing other religions as either false or inferior, Christianity should view them as worthy colleagues in the religious quest. In order to do this, Christians "must plunge resolutely into the great river of religions into which the streamlet of [their] own private inquiries have flowed."[2] Christians who do this discover, to their surprise, beliefs in other religions that are plausible. Consider, for example, reincarnation — the belief that we live multiple lives on this earth. Reincarnation, with the related belief in karma, is a presupposition of religions like Hinduism, Buddhism, and Sikhism. Many Christians view reincarnation as hocus-pocus. They reason as follows: "Reincarnation contends people die more than one time and are reborn more than one time. Yet the New Testament (Heb 9:27) teaches we die only once. After death comes the judgment. Therefore, reincarnation — which is contrary to Heb 9:27 — is a spurious belief." Christians can view reincarnation as hocus-pocus as long as they do not take time to investigate evidence supporting reincarnation. Every inquisitive Christian should read *There Is a River: The Story of Edgar Cayce* by Thomas Sugrue.[3] *There Is a River* is a biography of Edgar Cayce, the Kentucky psychic, who (raised a Southern Baptist) stumbled into a belief in reincarnation. This book "turned me around" as far as the possibility of reincarnation is concerned. Every inquisitive Christian should read the chapter entitled "Reincarnation and Renewed Chances" in Leslie Weatherhead's book entitled *The Christian Agnostic.*[4] Or read the anthology on reincarnation compiled by Joseph Head and S. L. Cranston entitled *Reincarnation: The Phoenix Fire Mystery.*[5] On a popular level is the book by Morey Bernstein entitled *The Search for Bridey Murphy.*[6] Over six million copies have been sold of Bernstein's book, which tells of a Colorado housewife who recalls details of a life previously lived in Ireland. I sometimes wish that Christians who reject reincarnation out-of-hand could listen to some of the students I have taught in my comparative religion classes. One of the evidences for reincarnation is the déjà vu phenomenon — the feeling that one has seen or heard something before. Students have told me about their déjà vu experiences. I shall never forget an older female student, specializing in library science, whose husband was in the military. She told me of a visit she made years before to Mt. Vernon, George Washington's home, while her husband was stationed in the District of Columbia. She related that when she and her husband started walking toward the front entrance of Mt. Vernon she was overwhelmed with the feeling "I have been here before." She could visualize the layout of the rooms inside George Washington's home. She found this intuition so discombobulating she refused to enter the house. "I told my husband to go ahead by himself. I went back to our car and waited for him. This déjà vu experience was too heavy for me to handle."

Interpreting and reinterpreting the Christian faith is an unending task for the church. Across the centuries Christianity as a belief system has been reshaped or reinterpreted many times. These interpretations have occurred within changing cultural contexts. The cultural context within which Thomas Aquinas expounded the Christian faith for the thirteenth century is not identical to the cultural context within which John Calvin interpreted the Christian faith for the city of Geneva in the sixteenth century. Here at the beginning of the third millennium those of us who call ourselves Christians find ourselves living in an unprecedented cultural context. As a result of contemporary means of travel and communication the world has become a global village. I concede the phrase "global village" is trite, but this phrase does capture the insight that — thinking figuratively — the world has become smaller and smaller. In this global village it is inevitable that Christians rub shoulders with devotees of other religions. For Christians to be receptive to beliefs, like reincarnation, emphasized by other religions does not mean they are abandoning or betraying Christianity. Rather they are appropriating insights previously unavailable to them.

Thus, there are four strategies that thinking Christians can use to rescue Jesus from unthinking Christians. First of all, they should accept and rejoice in religious pluralism. By so doing they can appropriate alternative religious beliefs which are plausible but which orthodox Christianity either rejects or refuses to consider. The view that ideally there should be one, and only one, universal religion is naive. Humankind's diversity makes this impossible. Moreover, the view that God, the cosmic power, has dealt with only one segment of humanity, the Christians, is provincial and audacious. Evocative religious figures (Muhammad in the Middle East; Siddhartha Gautama — the Buddha — in Asia; Lao-tzu and Confucius in China; Nanak in the Punjab; Mahavira in India) exist in cultures outside western culture. Cultural conditioning undoubtedly plays a strategic role in determining which religious figure various people hold in esteem. Instead of major religions competing with one another, should not they pool their resources to alleviate human suffering? Secondly, reflective Christians should avoid both lollipop conceptions of Jesus ("He is my dearest friend") and aggrandizing conceptions that transform him into a remote, ethereal figure far removed from what people experience in their day-to-day existence. Thirdly, reflective disciples must remember they are under no obligation to accept everything earlier generations of Christians have believed. In this regard I have argued they would do well to abandon the cruxification of the Christian religion. To contend Jesus' crucifixion was a sin sacrifice is no longer credible. Fourthly, reflective Christians should distinguish the post-resurrection Jesus from the pre-resurrection Jesus, the historical Jesus from the risen Christ. The church has tended to blend these two. This blending has made it impossible for believers to have a realistic understanding of the historical Jesus. That the historical Jesus had expectations that were erroneous does not nullify his resurrection from the dead. Nor have his erroneous beliefs diminished the influence he has had on multitudes of people. The figure of Jesus, the carpenter from Nazareth, possesses an evocative, radioactive, magnetic power, particularly in the Western world, far exceeding the influence of worthies like Socrates. Jesus' evocative power is an endowment granted by none other than God himself.

Notes

1. Roland H. Bainton, *Christianity* (American Heritage Library; Boston: Houghton Mifflin, 1964), 354.
2. Pierre Teilhard de Chardin, *How I Believe* (New York: Harper & Row, 1969), 61–62.
3. Thomas Sugrue, *There Is a River: The Story of Edgar Cayce* (Denver: A. R. E. Publishing House, 1989).
4. Leslie D. Weatherhead, *The Christian Agnostic* (Nashville: Abingdon, 1965), 293–316.
5. Joseph Head and S. L. Cranston, *Reincarnation: The Phoenix Fire Mystery* (New York: Julian Press/Crown, 1977).
6. I concede that Bernstein's book is viewed with contempt by academics. The reason for this academic contempt is obvious: the book does not abound with erudite footnotes and obscure Latin phrases. A sympathetic treatment of reincarnation from a Jewish viewpoint can be found in *Does the Soul Survive?* by Rabbi Elie Kaplan Spitz (Woodstock, Vt.: Jewish Lights, 2001). This book is superb.

Chapter 12

In Conclusion

If it could ever be proved that the Gospels consisted throughout of completely accurate material for a biography of Jesus, the traditional Christian faith would collapse in ruins. This can hardly be stressed too strongly, especially to those Christians who are convinced that an orthodox faith rests on the factual reliability of the Bible in general and on the status of the Gospels in particular as precise records of the words and acts of Jesus, and of the incidents of his life. Such a conviction is very nearly the reverse of the truth. Every one of the systematic edifices of belief, both orthodox and heretical, which have marked the history of Christianity has depended in the last analysis on an edited, expanded, or artificially interpreted version of the Gospel text.[1]

These words were not written by an atheist or cynic. Instead, they were written by John Austin Baker, an English clergyman identified with Corpus Christi College of Oxford University. From the first century to the present Christian interpreters have constructed "systematic edifices of belief." These edifices include everything from Augustine's *City of God* to Thomas Aquinas's *Summa Theologiae* to John Calvin's *Institutes of the Christian Religion* to Karl Barth's *Church Dogmatics*. All of these theologians are to be admired; they meant well. Yet their interpretations of the Christian faith vary. No two are alike. This variability is understandable. The foundation of the Christian faith is the Christ event: the life, death, and resurrection of the carpenter from Nazareth. But what God accomplished in Jesus is not obvious. The significance of Jesus for others is not self-evident. This absence explains why the first generation of Christian interpreters had multiple and different understandings of Jesus' significance. The Fourth Gospel presents one understanding of Jesus' significance. Paul's letter to the Romans presents another understanding. The letter to the Hebrews presents still another. This diversity shows there was never one original Christian gospel. The identity of early Christianity is problematical. This puzzle of the identity of Christianity has continued to the present day. Hence the poignant question posed by Dietrich Bonhoeffer: "Who is Jesus Christ for us today?"[2] Bonhoeffer raised this question in a letter that he wrote from prison several months before being hanged by the Nazis.

Scores of people today couldn't care less about Bonhoeffer's question. The reason for this lack of concern is obvious; our age is a secular age. The pursuit of wealth and devotion to pleasure preoccupy many who consequently have a narcotic indifference toward religion.

Yet scores of people do care about Bonhoeffer's question: "Who is Jesus Christ for us today?" The words that immediately follow are written for them. In grappling with Bonhoeffer's question we must bear in mind that some questions cannot be answered with certainty or precision. However, this lack of certainty or precision does not mean the questions are foolish. There exists what can be labeled the "interrogative dilemma": the capacity of the mind to ask questions that it does not have the capacity to answer. Immanuel Kant recognized this interrogative dilemma when he wrote: "Human reason has this peculiar fate, that in one species of its knowledge it is burdened by questions which, as prescribed by the very nature of reason itself, it is not able to ignore, but which, as transcending all its powers, it is not able to answer."[3] Thus questions without obvious answers abound. Consider Martin Heidegger's question: "Why is there anything rather than nothing?"[4] Heidegger's question may be the most fundamental question of all; why does anything exist? Why not nothingness? Or consider Albert Camus's question:

"What is the meaning of life?"[5] Unanswerable questions continue. What happens to us when we die? Why do the innocent suffer? To what goal is the human race's pilgrimage headed? To express this question another way: humankind has passed from the Stone Age to the space age but where, pray tell, is humankind going to end up? And then there is the agonizing question of evil. Assuming God is just and good (a heavenly Father), why does God permit evil to exist in a world he created? Why didn't God intervene in the preceding, cruel century when over a million infants and children were slaughtered in the presence of their parents by the Nazis? Where was God when twenty million people were killed in the context of the Second World War? Why does God permit the savage tribal wars of black Africa to continue? Why famine, drought, sickness, and pestilence? Why are infants born physically and mentally deformed? Does demonic power reside in God himself? In this regard I refer to the most ignored verse in the Bible: "Now the Spirit of the Lord departed from Saul, and an evil spirit from the Lord tormented him" (1 Sam 16:14). On the judgment day, taking into account this world's excess of natural evil, who should be put on trial? God or humankind? Moreover, doesn't this world's excess of undeserved human suffering make understandable Robert Frost's couplet:

> Forgive, O Lord, my little jokes on Thee,
> And I'll forgive Thy great big one on me.

Questions posed in the preceding paragraph are sensible. But Christianity provides no answers to them. Neither does human reason. Our puzzlement over these questions is intensified by our post-Hubble recognition that we live in an expanding universe. The universe is exploding outwardly at a fantastic speed in all directions. Seventeenth-century philosopher Blaise Pascal anticipated our contemporary cosmic discombobulation when he placed on the lips of an unreasonable doubter the following words:

I know not who put me into the world, nor what the world is, nor what I myself am. I am in terrible ignorance of everything. I know not what my body is, nor my senses, nor my soul, not even that part of me which thinks what I say, which reflects on all and on itself, and knows itself no more than the rest. I see those frightful spaces of the universe which surround me, and I find myself tied to one corner of this vast expanse, without knowing why I am put in this place rather than in another, nor why the short time which is given me to live is assigned to me at this point rather than at another of the whole eternity which was before me or which shall come after me. I see nothing but infinites on all sides, which surround me as an atom, and as a shadow which endures only for an instant and returns no more. All I know is that I must soon die, but what I know least is this very death which I cannot escape.[6]

Yet in the midst of this infinite universe and this whirlwind of unanswerable questions scores of people get up every morning and confront the challenges of the day: going to work, taking care of children, looking after elderly parents, relating to spouses, meeting household responsibilities, paying bills, experiencing physical suffering, and enduring life, which, in the words of Clarence Darrow, is "a serious burden, which no thinking, humane person would wantonly inflict on some one else."[7] Darrow's observation calls to mind Albert Schweitzer's remark that he could scarcely remember a day he was glad to be alive. Darrow's observation also calls to mind Aunt Elner's remark in Fannie Flagg's novel *Welcome to the World, Baby Girl!* Aunt Elner observed, "Poor little old human beings — they're jerked into this world without having any idea where they came from or what it is they are supposed to do, or how long they have to do it in. Or where they are gonna wind up after that. But bless their hearts, most of them wake up every morning and keep on trying to make some sense out of it. Why, you can't help but love them, can you? I just wonder why more of them aren't as crazy as betsy bugs."[8] In other words, God has placed people on this earth for a journey but has not provided them with a map.

But also in the midst of this maelstrom of unanswered questions is the Christ event: the obstinate historical fact that some two thousand years ago a Jew named Jesus lived on this earth. He was "more" than a man. What that "more" was is difficult to define. He taught, was crucified, was raised from the dead and continues to live in the spirit world. Centuries ago Simmias, a contemporary of Socrates, recognized the need for a raft upon which to ride the seas of life.[9] As inquisitive Christians we can gratefully seize the Christ event as our raft upon which to navigate life's seas. We can pray to God as Jesus' disciples. We can learn of Jesus' life by meditating on the Gospels. A careful study of the Gospels can lead some — but not all — to conclude that the historical Jesus on occasion was not a likable person; a person's significance, however, is not dependent upon likability. His Golden Rule ("Treat other people as you would want to be treated") can be our moral compass in dealing with other people. His resurrection from the dead can be the basis for our hope in a blessed future life. And through it all we can live in reverent awe of the heavenly Father (the God of Abraham, Isaac, Jacob, and Jesus) and as an antidote to pride, we can constantly bear in mind our fragility, contingency, and transitoriness.

One concluding remark: inquisitive Christians tend to be loners and mavericks. Their tendency toward lone-rangerism leads some to conclude they can do without the church. "I can be a Christian without going to church on Sunday." This attitude is unfortunate. The contemporary church needs thinking Christians. Such is the case because in many places the church, plagued by theological anarchy, is a wounded institution. The church has been damaged by this era's secular zeitgeist, by manipulative televangelists who dress like Las Vegas casino rock stars and dispense religious froth, and by fundamentalists who know but do not think. Unfortunately, these wounded churches have a way on occasion of breaking a person's heart.[10] Yet we must remember that ultimately the church belongs to God. It is the body of Christ characterized by benevolent deeds — maintaining hospitals, soup kitchens, orphanages, hospices, homes for unwed mothers, places of refuge for the homeless. Churches fulfill compassionate roles in society few other organizations fulfill. How many soup kitchens or places of refuge for the homeless are maintained by the American Philosophical Society? Thus thinking Christians, I believe, can play a role in helping wounded churches become what they should be. And they can play a role in reawakening within the intelligentsia, which has largely abandoned organized Christianity, an interest in the Christian faith.

Notes

1. John Austin Baker, *The Foolishness of God* (London: Darton, Longman & Todd, 1970), 137.

2. Dietrich Bonhoeffer, *Letters and Papers from Prison* (London: SCM, 1967), 139.

3. Immanuel Kant, *Critique of Pure Reason* (Old Tappan, N.J.: Macmillan, 1956), 7.

4. Martin Heidegger, *An Introduction to Metaphysics* (trans. Ralph Manheim; New York: Anchor Books, 1961), 1–2.

5. Albert Camus, *The Myth of Sisyphus and Other Essays* (trans. Justin O'Brien; New York: Knopf, 1955), 3–4.

6. Blaise Pascal, *Pensées: The Provincial Letters* (trans. W. F. Trotter and Thomas M'Crie; New York: Modern Library, 1941), 68.

7. Clarence Darrow, *The Story of My Life* (New York: Charles Scribner's Sons, 1932), 395. Our thirst for immortality is puzzling. If it be true that life is a "serious burden" because of such factors as aging, physical and mental suffering, and encounters with evil, then why do people desire *another* life? There is no reason a priori why suffering and evil and tragedy are not also features of a future existence.

8. Fannie Flagg, *Welcome to the World, Baby Girl!* (New York: Ballantine, 1998).

9. This "raft" remark appears in the *Phaedo*. See Plato, *Plato: The Collected Dialogues* (ed. Edith Hamilton and Huntington Cairns; Princeton, N.J.: Princeton University Press, 1961), 68.

10. I was raised within the Southern Baptist denomination. My fate has been to see this largest of Protestant denominations torn asunder by the fundamentalist controversy. Fundamentalists now control the denomination, and Baptists sympathetic to post-Enlightenment scholarship have been expelled. I have witnessed this controversy with great sorrow and dismay.

Appendix A

A Listing of All References to Kingdom in the Synoptic Gospels

Sayings That Either Emphasize the Nearness of the Kingdom or Present the Kingdom as a Future Hope

Matt 3:1–2 In those days came John the Baptist, preaching in the wilderness of Judea, "Repent, for the *kingdom of heaven* is at hand."

Matt 4:17 From that time Jesus began to preach, saying, "Repent, for the *kingdom of heaven* is at hand."

Matt 6:10a "Thy *kingdom* come."

Matt 10:7 And preach as you go saying, "The *kingdom of heaven* is at hand."

Matt 12:28 "But if it is by the Spirit of God that I cast out demons, then the *kingdom of God* has come upon you."

Matt 16:28 "Truly, I say to you, there are some standing here who will not taste death before they see the Son of Man coming in his *kingdom*."

Matt 25:34 Then the King will say to those at his right hand, "Come, O blessed of my Father, inherit the *kingdom* prepared for you from the foundation of the world."

Mark 1:14–15 Now after John was arrested, Jesus came into Galilee, preaching the gospel of God and saying, "The time is fulfilled, and the *kingdom of God* is at hand; repent, and believe in the gospel."

Mark 9:1 And he said to them, "Truly, I say to you, there are some standing here who will not taste death before they see the *kingdom of God* come with power."

Mark 11:10 "Blessed be the *kingdom* of our father David that is coming! Hosanna in the highest!"

Mark 15:43 Joseph of Arimathea, a respected member of the council, who was also himself looking for the *kingdom of God,* took courage and went to Pilate, and asked for the body of Jesus.

Luke 9:27 "But I tell you truly, there are some standing here who will not taste of death before they see the *kingdom of God*."

Luke 10:9 "Heal the sick in it and say to them, 'The *kingdom of God* has come near you.'"

127

Luke 10:11 "Even the dust of your own town that clings to our feet, we wipe off against you; nevertheless know this, that the *kingdom of God* has come near."

Luke 11:2 And he said to them "When you pray, say: Father, hallowed be thy name. Thy *kingdom* come."

Luke 11:20 "But if it is by the finger of God that I cast out demons, then the *kingdom of God* has come upon you."

Luke 19:11 As they heard these things, he proceeded to tell a parable, because he was near to Jerusalem, and because they supposed that the *kingdom of God* was to appear immediately.

Luke 21:31 "So also when you see these things taking place, you know that the *kingdom of God* is near."

Luke 23:42 And he said, "Jesus, remember me when you come in your *kingdom*."

Luke 23:50–51 Now there was a man named Joseph from the Jewish town of Arimathea. He was a member of the council, a good and righteous man, who had not consented to their purpose and deed, and he was looking for the *kingdom of God*.

Sayings Dealing with Eating, Drinking, and Sitting in the Kingdom

Matt 8:11–12 "I tell you, many will come from east and west and sit at table with Abraham, Isaac, and Jacob in the *kingdom of heaven*, while the sons of the kingdom will be thrown into the outer darkness; there men will weep and gnash their teeth."

Matt 26:29 "I tell you I shall not drink again of this fruit of the vine until that day when I drink it new with you in my Father's *kingdom*."

Mark 14:25 "Truly, I say to you, I shall not drink again of the fruit of the vine until that day when I drink it new in the *kingdom of God*."

Luke 13:29 "And many will come from east and west, and from north and south, and sit at table in the *kingdom of God*."

Luke 14:15 When one of those who sat at table with him heard this, he said to him, "Blessed is he who shall eat bread in the *kingdom of God*."

Luke 22:15–18 And he said to them, "I have earnestly desired to eat this Passover with you before I suffer; for I tell you I shall not eat it until it is fulfilled in the *kingdom of God*." And he took a cup, and when he had given thanks he said, "Take this, and divide it among yourselves; for I tell you that from now on I shall not drink of the fruit of the vine until the *kingdom of God* comes."

Luke 22:28–30 "You are those who have continued with me in my trials; as my Father appointed a *kingdom* for me, so do I appoint for you that you may eat and drink at my table in my *kingdom*, and sit on thrones judging the twelve tribes of Israel."

Sayings Presenting the Kingdom as an Object of Vision

Matt 16:28 "Truly I say to you, there are some standing here who will not taste death before they see the Son of Man coming in his *kingdom.*"

Mark 9:1 "Truly I say to you there are some standing here who will not taste death before they see the *kingdom of God* come with power."

Luke 9:27 "But I tell you truly, there are some standing here who will not taste of death before they see the *kingdom of God.*"

Luke 13:28 "There you will weep and gnash your teeth, when you see Abraham and Isaac and Jacob and all the prophets in the *kingdom of God* and you yourselves thrust out."

Sayings Concerned with Status in the Kingdom

Matt 5:19 "Whosoever then relaxes one of the least of these commandments and teaches men so, shall be called least in the *kingdom of heaven;* but he who does them and teaches them shall be called great in the *kingdom of heaven.*"

Matt 11:11 "Truly, I say to you, among those born of women there has risen no one greater than John the Baptist; yet he who is least in the *kingdom of heaven* is greater than he."

Matt 18:1, 4 At that time the disciples came to Jesus, saying, "Who is the greatest in the *kingdom of heaven?*" . . . "Whoever humbles himself like this child, he is the greatest in the *kingdom of heaven.*"

Matt 20:21 And he said to her, "What do you want?" She said to him, "Command that these two sons of mine may sit, one at your right hand and one at your left in your *kingdom.*"

Luke 7:28 "I tell you, among those born of women none is greater than John; yet he who is least in the *kingdom of God* is greater than he."

Luke 22:28–30 "You are those who have continued with me in my trials; as my Father appointed a *kingdom* for me, so do I appoint for you that you may eat and drink at my table in my *kingdom,* and sit on thrones judging the twelve tribes of Israel."

The Entry Sayings

Matt 5:20 "For I tell you, unless you righteousness exceeds that of the scribes and Pharisees, you will never enter the *kingdom of heaven.*"

Matt 7:21 "Not every one who says to me, 'Lord, Lord,' shall enter the *kingdom of heaven,* but he who does the will of my Father who is in heaven."

Matt 18:1–3 At that time the disciples came to Jesus, saying, "Who is the greatest in the *kingdom of heaven?*" And calling him a child, he put him in the midst of them, and said, "Truly, I say to you, unless you turn and become like children, you will never enter the *kingdom of heaven.*"

Matt 19:23–24 And Jesus said to his disciples, "Truly, I say to you, it will be hard for a rich man to enter the *kingdom of heaven*. Again, I tell you, it is easier for a camel to go through the eye of a needle than for a rich man to enter the *kingdom of heaven.*"

Matt 21:31b Jesus said to them, "Truly, I say to you, the tax collectors and the harlots go into the *kingdom of God* before you."

Matt 23:13 "But woe to you, scribes and Pharisees, hypocrites! because you shut *the kingdom of heaven* against men; for you neither enter yourselves, nor allow those who would enter to go in."

Mark 9:47 "And if your eye causes you to sin, pluck it out; it is better for you to enter the *kingdom of God* with one eye than with two eyes to be thrown into hell."

Mark 10:23–25 And Jesus looked around and said to his disciples, "How hard it will be for those who have riches to enter the *kingdom of God!*" And the disciples were amazed at his word. But Jesus said to them again, "Children, how hard it is to enter the *kingdom of God!* It is easier for a camel to go through the eye of a needle than for a rich man to enter the *kingdom of God.*"

Luke 18:17 "Truly, I say to you, whoever does not receive the *kingdom of God* like a child shall not enter it."

Luke 18:24–25 Jesus looking at him said, "How hard it is for those who have riches to enter the *kingdom of God!* For it is easier for a camel to go through the eye of a needle than for a rich man to enter the *kingdom of God.*"

The Kingdom as the Object of a Proclamation

Matt 4:23 And he went about all Galilee, teaching in their synagogues and preaching the gospel of the *kingdom* and healing every disease and every infirmity among the people.

Matt 9:35 And Jesus went about all the cities and villages, teaching in their synagogues and preaching the gospel of the *kingdom,* and healing every disease and every infirmity.

Matt 24:14 "And this gospel of the *kingdom* will be preached throughout the whole world, as a testimony to all nations; and then the end will come."

Luke 4:43 But he said to them, "I must preach the good news of the *kingdom of God* to the other cities also; for I was sent for this purpose."

Luke 8:1 Soon after he went on through cities and villages, preaching and bringing the good news of the *kingdom of God.*

Luke 9:1–2 And he called the twelve together and gave them power and authority over all demons and to cure diseases, and he sent them out to preach the *kingdom of God* and to heal.

Luke 9:11b He welcomed them and spoke to them of the *kingdom of God,* and cured those who had need of healing.

Luke 9:60 But he said to him, "Leave the dead to bury their own dead; but as for you, go and proclaim the *kingdom of God.*"

Luke 16:16 "The law and the prophets were until John; since then the good news of the *kingdom of God* is preached."

The Parables of the Kingdom

Matt 13:19 "When anyone hears the word of the *kingdom* and does not understand it, the evil one comes and snatches away what is sown in his heart."

Matt 13:24 Another parable he put before them, saying, "The *kingdom of heaven* may be compared to a man who sowed good seed in his field."

Matt 13:31 Another parable he put before them, saying, "The *kingdom of heaven* is like a grain of mustard seed which a man took and sowed in his field."

Matt 13:33 He told them another parable. "The *kingdom of heaven* is like leaven which a woman took and hid in three measures of meal, till it was all leavened."

Matt 13:38a "The field is the world, and the good seed means the sons of the *kingdom.*"

Matt 13:41 "The Son of Man will send his angels, and they will gather out of his *kingdom* all causes of sin and all evildoers."

Matt 13:43a "Then the righteous will shine like the sun in the *kingdom* of their Father."

Matt 13:44a "The *kingdom of heaven* is like treasure hidden in a field, which a man found and covered up."

Matt 13:45 "Again, the *kingdom of heaven* is like a merchant in search of fine pearls."

Matt 13:47 "Again, the *kingdom of heaven* is like a net which was thrown into the sea and gathered fish of every kind."

Matt 18:23 "Therefore the *kingdom of heaven* may be compared to a king who wished to settle accounts with his servants."

Matt 20:1 "For the *kingdom of heaven* is like a householder who went out early in the morning to hire laborers for his vineyard."

Matt 22:2 "The *kingdom of heaven* may be compared to a king who gave a marriage feast for his son."

Matt 25:1 "Then the *kingdom of heaven* shall be compared to ten maidens who took their lamps and went out to meet the bridegroom."

Mark 4:26 And he said, "The *kingdom of God* is as if a man should scatter seed upon the ground."

Mark 4:30–31a And he said, "With what can we compare the *kingdom of God,* or what parable shall we use for it? It is like a grain of mustard seed."

Luke 13:18–19a He said therefore, "What is the *kingdom of God* like? And to what shall I compare it? It is like a grain of mustard seed which a man took and sowed in his garden."

Luke 13:20–21 And again he said, "To what shall I compare the *kingdom of God?* It is like leaven which a woman took and hid in three measures of meal, till it was all leavened."

Miscellaneous Passages

Matt 5:3 "Blessed are the poor in spirit, for theirs is the *kingdom of heaven.*"

Matt 5:10 "Blessed are those who are persecuted for righteousness sake, for theirs is the *kingdom of heaven.*"

Matt 6:33 "But seek first his *kingdom* and his righteousness, and all these things shall be yours as well."

Matt 11:12 "From the days of John the Baptist until now the *kingdom of heaven* has suffered violence, and men of violence take it by force."

Matt 13:11 And he answered them, "To you it has been given to know the secrets of the *kingdom of heaven,* but to them it has not been given."

Matt 13:52 And he said to them, "Therefore every scribe who has been trained for the *kingdom of heaven* is like a householder who brings out of his treasure what is new and what is old."

Matt 16:19a "I will give you the keys of the *kingdom of heaven.*"

Matt 19:12b "There are eunuchs who have made themselves eunuchs for the sake of the *kingdom of heaven.* He who is able to receive this, let him receive it."

Matt 19:14 Jesus said, "Let the children come to me, and do not hinder them; for to such belongs the *kingdom of heaven.*"

Matt 21:43 "Therefore I tell you, the *kingdom of God* will be taken away from you and given to a nation producing the fruits of it."

Mark 4:11 And he said to them, "To you has been given the secret of the *kingdom of God,* but for those outside everything is in parables."

Mark 10:14–15 But when Jesus saw it he was indignant, and said to them, "Let the children come to me, do not hinder them; for to such belongs the *kingdom of God.* Truly, I say to you, whoever does not receive the *kingdom of God* like a child shall not enter it."

Mark 12:34 And when Jesus saw that he answered wisely, he said to him, "You are not far from the *kingdom of God.*"

Luke 6:20b "Blessed are you poor, for yours is the *kingdom of heaven.*"

Luke 8:10a "To you it has been given to know the secrets of the *kingdom of God.*"

Luke 9:62 Jesus said to him, "No one who puts his hand to the plow and looks back is fit for the *kingdom of God.*"

Luke 12:31 "Instead, seek his *kingdom,* and these things shall be yours as well."

Luke 12:32 "Fear not, little flock, for it is your Father's good pleasure to give you the *kingdom.*"

Luke 17:20–21 Being asked by the Pharisees when the *kingdom of God* was coming, he answered them, "The *kingdom of God* is not coming with signs to be observed; nor will they say, 'Lo, here it is!' or 'There!' for behold, the *kingdom of God* is in the midst of you." This verse, usually translated "The kingdom of God is within you," is dealt with in Appendix C.

Luke 18:16 But Jesus called them to him, saying, "Let the children come to me, and do not hinder them; for to such belongs the *kingdom of God.*"

Luke 18:29–30 And he said to them, "Truly, I say to you, there is no man who has left house or wife or brothers or parents or children, for the sake of the *kingdom of God,* who will not receive manifold more in this time, and in the age to come, eternal life."

Sayings That Refer to a Kingdom, but Not to the Kingdom of God

Matt 4:8 Again, the devil took him to a very high mountain, and showed him all the *kingdoms* of the world and the glory of them.

Matt 12:25–26 Knowing their thoughts, he said to them, "Every *kingdom* divided against itself is laid waste, and no city or house divided against itself will stand; and if Satan casts out Satan, he is divided against himself; how then will his *kingdom* stand?"

Matt 24:7a "For nation will rise against nation, and *kingdom* against *kingdom.*"

Mark 3:24 "If a *kingdom* is divided against itself, that *kingdom* cannot stand."

Mark 6:23 And he vowed to her, "Whatever you ask me, I will give you, even half of my *kingdom.*"

Mark 13:8a "For nation will rise against nation, and *kingdom* against *kingdom.*"

Luke 4:5 And the devil took him up, and showed him all the *kingdoms* of the world in a moment of time.

Luke 11:17–18a But he, knowing their thought, said to them, "Every *kingdom* divided against itself is laid waste, and house falls upon house. And if Satan is also divided against himself, how will his *kingdom* stand?"

Luke 19:12 He said therefore, "A nobleman went into a far country to receive a *kingdom* and then return."

Luke 19:15a When he returned, having received the *kingdom,* he commanded these servants, to whom he had given the money, to be called.

Luke 21:10 Then he said to them, "Nation will rise against nation, and *kingdom* against *kingdom.*"

Appendix B

The Kingdom of God
in Patristic Literature

The New Testament was not the only document produced by the early church. In fact, some early Christians were prolific authors. Christian documents written immediately after the New Testament are collectively referred to as patristic literature, i.e., the writings of the Fathers (*patres*) of the church from the end of the first century through the eighth century. These writings are a gold mine for understanding what Christians believed during the opening centuries of the Christian movement.[1]

There is reason to assume a continuity between Jesus' proclamation of the kingdom of God and the understanding of the kingdom found in patristic literature. A study of this literature reveals that early Christian writers thought of the kingdom as a place and as a future hope. Representative patristic authors will now be cited.

The Evidence of the Apostolic Fathers

References to the kingdom in the Apostolic Fathers are not numerous. Nonetheless, the references that do occur portray the kingdom as a future hope.

1 Clement

Penned toward the close of Diocletian's persecution, this epistle was written in the name of the Roman Church to the Christian brotherhood in Corinth. Clement, bishop of the Roman Christians, wrote the following regarding the kingdom:

The Apostles received the Gospel for us from the Lord Jesus Christ; Jesus Christ was sent forth from God. So then Christ is from God, and the Apostles are from Christ. Both therefore came of the will of God in the appointed order. Having therefore received a charge, and having been fully assured through the resurrection of our Lord Jesus Christ and confirmed in the word of God with full assurance of the Holy Ghost, they went forth with the glad tidings that the Kingdom of God *should come.* (*1 Clem.* 42:1–3; italics added)

All the generations from Adam unto this day have passed away; but they that by God's grace were perfected in love dwell in the abode of the pious; and they shall be made manifest in the visitation of the Kingdom of God. For it is written: Enter into the closet for a very little while, until my anger and my wrath shall pass away, and I will remember a good day and will raise you from your tombs.

(*1 Clem* 50:2–4)

The preceding quotation collocates the coming of the kingdom and the resurrection from the dead. The futuristic implication is obvious.

2 Clement

In *2 Clement,* an ancient homily dating from about 120 to 140 C.E., the following references to the kingdom appear.

Wherefore, brethren, let us forsake our sojourn in this world and do the will of Him that called us, and let us not be afraid to depart out of this world. For the Lord saith, "Ye shall be as lambs in the midst of wolves." But Peter answered and said unto him, "What then, if the wolves should tear the lambs?" Jesus said unto Peter, "Let not the lambs fear the wolves after they are dead; and ye also, fear ye not them that kill you and are not able to do anything to you; but fear him that after ye are dead hath power over soul and body, to cast them into the Gehenna of fire. *And ye know, brethren, that the sojourn of this flesh in this world is mean and for a short time, but the promise of Christ is great and marvelous, even the rest of the Kingdom that shall be and of life eternal.* What then can we do to obtain them, but walk in holiness and righteousness, and consider these worldly things as alien to us, and not desire them.["] (*2 Clem.* 5:1–6; italics added)

And let not any one of you say that this flesh is not judged neither riseth again. Understand ye. In what were ye saved? In what did ye recover your sight? If ye were not in the flesh. We ought therefore to guard the flesh as a temple of God; for in like manner as ye were called in the flesh, he shall come also in the flesh. If Christ the Lord who saved us, being first spirit, then became flesh and so called us, in like manner also shall we in this flesh receive our reward. Let us therefore love one another, that we all may come into the Kingdom of God. (*2 Clem.* 9:1–6)

Wherefore, my brethren, let us not be double-minded but endure patiently in hope, that we may also obtain our reward. For faithful is he that promised to pay to each man the recompense of his works. If therefore we shall have wrought righteousness in the sight of God, we shall enter into his Kingdom and shall receive the promises which ear hath not heard nor eye seen, neither hath it entered into the heart of man. (*2 Clem.* 11:5–7)

Let us therefore *await the Kingdom of God* betimes in love and righteousness, since *we know not the day of* God's appearing. For the Lord himself, being asked by a certain person when his Kingdom would come, said, "When the two shall be one, and the outside as inside, and the male with the female, neither male nor female." Now the two are one, when we speak truth among ourselves, and in two bodies there shall be one soul without dissimulation. And by "the outside as the inside" he meaneth this: by the inside he meaneth the soul and by the outside the body. Therefore in like manner as thy body appeareth, so also let the soul be manifest in its good works. And by "the male with the female, neither male or female," he meaneth this: that a brother seeing a sister should have no thought of her as a female, and that a sister seeing a brother should have no thought of him as a male. These things if he do, the Kingdom of my Father *shall come.* (*2 Clem.* 12:1–6; italics added)

In these quotations the kingdom is obviously a future hope.

The Epistle of Polycarp to the Philippians

In the *Epistle of Polycarp to the Philippians* a reference to the kingdom appears in the context of ethical exhortations.

In like manner also the younger men must be blameless in all things, caring for purity before everything and curbing themselves from every evil. For it is a good thing to refrain from lusts in the world, for every lust warreth against the Spirit and neither whoremongers nor effeminate persons nor defilers of themselves with men shall inherit the Kingdom of God, neither they that do untoward things.

(Pol. *Phil.* 5:3)

The closing part of the preceding quotation reflects 1 Cor 6:9–10; the futuristic reference to the kingdom is obvious.

The Didache

The two references to the kingdom in the *Didache* are of interest because of the distinction made between kingdom and church.

But as touching the eucharistic thanksgiving give ye thanks thus. First, as regards the cup: We give Thee thanks, O our Father, for the holy vine of Thy son David, which Thou madest known unto us through Thy Son Jesus; Thine is the glory for ever and ever. As this broken bread was scattered upon the mountains and being gathered together became one, so may Thy Church be gathered together from the ends of the earth into Thy Kingdom; for Thine is the glory and the power through Jesus Christ for ever and ever. (*Did.* 9:1–4)

Remember, Lord, Thy Church to deliver it from all evil and to perfect it in Thy love; and gather it together from the four winds — even the Church which has been sanctified — into Thy Kingdom which Thou hast prepared for it. (*Did.* 11:5)

In these *Didache* quotations the kingdom is conceived as the goal of the church.

The Epistle of Barnabas

The Epistle of Barnabas teaches that the resurrection's purpose is the glorification of Christians in the kingdom of God.

It is good therefore to learn the ordinances of the Lord, as many as have been written above, and to walk in them. For he that doeth these things shall be glorified in the Kingdom of God; whereas he that chooseth their opposites shall perish together with his works. For this cause is the resurrection, for this the recompense. I entreat those of you who are in higher station, if ye will receive any counsel of good advice from me, keep amongst you those to whom ye may do good. Fail not. The day is at hand, in which everything shall be destroyed together with the Evil One. The Lord is at hand and His reward. (*Barn.* 21:1–3)

Irenaeus

Irenaeus (ca. 142–200), for a number of years the Bishop of Lyons in Gaul, is primarily remembered for his anti-gnostic treatise *Against Heresies*. There are scores of places in *Against Heresies* where the kingdom was presented as a future hope and an object of sensory perception. Detailed attention, however, will be given to only one citation from this work. The citation includes Irenaeus's discussion of the predicted blessings of Gen 27:28–29. Irenaeus referred these blessings to the future kingdom of God. It would be difficult to conceive of the kingdom in more concrete terms than the following:

> The predicted blessing, therefore, belongs unquestionably to the times of the kingdom, when the righteous shall bear rule upon their rising from the dead; when also the creation, having been renovated and set free, shall fructify with an abundance of all kinds of food, from the dew of heaven, and from the fertility of the earth: as the elders who saw John, the disciple of the Lord, related that they had heard from him how the Lord used to teach in regard to these times, and say: The days will come, in which vines shall grow, each having ten thousand branches, and in each branch ten thousand twigs, and in each twig ten thousand shoots, and in each one of the shoots ten thousand clusters, and on every one of the clusters ten thousand grapes, and every grape when pressed will give five and twenty metretes of wine. And when any one of the saints shall lay hold of a cluster, another shall cry out, "I am a better cluster, take me; bless the Lord through me." In like manner [the Lord declared] that a grain of wheat would produce ten thousand ears, and that every ear should have ten thousand grains, and every grain would yield ten pounds of clear, pure, fine flour; and that all other fruit-bearing trees, and seeds and grass, would produce in similar proportions; and that all animals feeding [only] on the productions of the earth, should [in those days] become peaceful and harmonious among each other, and be in perfect subjection to man.
>
> And these things are borne witness to in writing by Papias, the hearer of John, and a companion of Polycarp, in his fourth book; for there are five books compiled by him. And he says in addition, "Now these things are credible to believers." And he says that, "when the traitor Judas did not give credit to them, and put the question, 'How then can things about to bring forth so abundantly be wrought by the Lord?' the Lord declared, 'They who shall come to

these [times] shall see.'" When prophesying of these times, therefore, Esaias says: "The wolf also shall feed with the lamb, and the leopard shall take his rest with the kid; the calf also, and the bull, and the lion shall eat together; and a little boy shall lead them. The ox and the bear shall feed together, and the lion shall eat straw as well as the ox. And the infant boy shall thrust his hand into the asp's den, into the nest also of the adder's brood; and they shall do no harm, nor have power to hurt anything in my holy mountain." And again he says, in recapitulation, "the lion shall eat straw like the ox, and the serpent earth as if it were bread; and they shall neither hurt nor annoy anything in my holy mountain, saith the Lord." (*Against Heresies* V.33.3–4)

Irenaeus protests all attempts to allegorize the sensory descriptions of the kingdom in these words,

Now all these things being such as they are, cannot be understood in reference to supercelestial matters; "for God," it is said, "will show to the whole earth that is under heaven thy glory." But in the times of the kingdom, the earth has been called again by Christ to its pristine condition, and Jerusalem rebuilt after the pattern of the Jerusalem above, of which the prophet Isaiah says, "Behold, I have depicted thy walls upon my hands, and thou art always in my sight." (*Against Heresies* V.34.2)

Tertullian

Because he was a prolific writer and the first ecclesiastic of prominence to use Latin, Tertullian (ca. 150–225) has been given the title of father of Latin theology.[2] In the writings of Tertullian, as in the writings of Irenaeus, the kingdom was conceived as a future hope.[3] For example, in his exegesis of the Pauline statement that "flesh and blood cannot inherit the Kingdom of God" Tertullian wrote,

How then is it, that the soul, which is the real author of the works of the flesh, shall attain to the kingdom of God, after the deeds done in the body have been atoned for, whilst the body, which was nothing but the soul's ministering agent, must remain in condemnation? Is the cup to be punished, but the poisoner to escape: Not that we indeed claim the kingdom of God for the flesh: all we do is, to assert a resurrection for the substance thereof, as the gate of the kingdom through which it is entered. But the resurrection is one thing, and the kingdom is another. *The resurrection is first, and afterwards the kingdom. We say, therefore, that the flesh rises again, but that when changed it obtains the kingdom.* "For the dead shall be raised incorruptible," even those who had been corruptible when their bodies fell into decay; "and we shall be changed, in a moment, in the twinkling of an eye. For this corruptible" — and as he spake, the apostle seemingly pointed to his own flesh — "must put on incorruption, and this mortal must put on immortality," in order, indeed, that it may be rendered a fit substance for the kingdom of God. "For we shall be like the angels." This will be the perfect change of our flesh — only after its resurrection. Now if, on the contrary, there is to be no flesh, how then shall it put on incorruption and immortality? Having then become something else by its change, it will obtain the kingdom of God, no longer the old flesh and blood, but the body which God shall have given it. Rightly then does the apostle declare, "Flesh and blood cannot inherit the kingdom of God"; for this honour does he ascribe to the changed condition which ensues on the resurrection. (*Against Marcion* 5.10)

This argument by Tertullian with reference to a transformation of the flesh reveals his concrete conception of the *basileia*. Note also the following extracts from his treatise *On the Resurrection of the Flesh.*

Now, if even parables obscure not the light of the gospel, how unlikely it is that plain sentences and declarations, which have an unmistakable meaning, should signify any other things than their literal sense! But it is by such declarations and sentences that the Lord sets forth either the last judgment, or the kingdom, or the resurrection: "It shall be more tolerable," He says, "for Tyre and Sidon in the day of judgment than for you." And, "Tell them that the kingdom of God is at hand," and again, "It shall be recompensed to you at the resurrection of the just." Now, if the mention of these events (I mean, the judgment day, and the kingdom of God, and the resurrection) has a plain and absolute sense, so that nothing about them can be pressed into an allegory, neither should those statements be forced into parables which describe the arrangement, and the process, and the experience of the kingdom of God, and of the judgment, and of the resurrection. On the contrary, things which are destined for the body should be carefully understood in a bodily sense, — not in a spiritual sense, as having nothing figurative in their nature. This is the reason why we have laid it down as a preliminary consideration, that the bodily substance both of the soul and of the flesh is liable to the recompense, which will have to be awarded in return for the cooperation of the two natures, that so the corporeality of the soul may not exclude the bodily nature of the flesh by suggesting a recourse to figurative descriptions, since both of them must needs be regarded as destined to take part in the kingdom, and the judgment, and the resurrection.

(*On the Resurrection* 33)

So, again, the very reclining at the feast in the kingdom of God, and sitting on Christ's thrones, and standing at last on His right hand and His left, and eating of the tree of life: what are all these but most certain proofs of a bodily appointment and destination? (*On the Resurrection* 35)

From these quotations it is evident Tertullian knew nothing of an abstract kingdom. Tertullian conceived of the kingdom in spatial terms.

Origen and Eusebius of Caesarea

Origen (ca. 185–254), the celebrated theologian of Alexandria and Caesarea, wrote from a philosophical standpoint that was essentially Platonic and Stoic. It is easy to understand, therefore, that although Origen conceived of the kingdom as future,[4] nonetheless there is the tendency for him to portray the kingdom as "spiritual" in nature.[5] But *indirectly* he is witness to the existence in the early church of a sensory-spatial understanding of the kingdom of God. Origen criticized those who do not understand that such statements as "Henceforth I shall not drink of this cup, until I drink it with you new in my father's Kingdom" should be taken *figuratively.* The following quotation from *First Principles* is cited in full.

Certain persons, then, refusing the labour of thinking, and adopting a superficial view of the letter of the law, and yielding rather in some measure to the indulgence of their own desires and lusts, being disciples of the letter alone, are of opinion that the fulfillment of the promises of the future are to be looked for in bodily pleasure and luxury; and therefore they especially desire to have again, after the resurrection, such bodily structures as may never be without the power of eating, and drinking, and performing all the functions of flesh and blood, not following the opinion of the Apostle Paul regarding the resurrection of a spiritual body. And consequently, they say, that after the resurrection there will be marriages, and begetting of children, imagining to themselves that the earthly city of Jerusalem is to be rebuilt, its foundations laid in precious stones, and its walls constructed of jasper, and its battlements of crystal; that it is to have a wall composed of many precious stones, as jasper, and sapphire, and chalcedony, and emerald, and sardonyx, and onyx, and chrysolite, and chrysophrase, and jacinth, and amethyst. Moreover, they think that the natives of other countries are to be given them as the ministers of their pleasures, whom they are to employ either as tillers of the field or builders of the walls, and by whom their ruined and fallen city is again to be raised up; and they think that they are to receive the wealth of the nations to live on, and that they will have control over their riches; that even the camels of Midian and Kedar will come, and bring to them gold, and incense, and precious stones. And these views they think to establish on the authority of the prophets by those promises which are written regarding Jerusalem; and by those passages also where it is said, that they who serve the Lord shall eat and drink, but that sinners shall hunger and thirst; that the righteous shall be joyful, but that sorrow shall possess the wicked. And from the New Testament also they quote the saying of the Savior, in which He makes a promise to His disciples concerning the joy of wine, saying, *Henceforth I shall not drink of this cup, until I drink it with you new in My Father's kingdom.*" They add, moreover, that declaration, in which the Savior calls those blessed who now hunger and thirst, promising them that they shall be satisfied; and many other scriptural illustrations are adduced by them, the meaning of which they do not perceive is to be taken figuratively. Then, again, agreeably to the form of things in this life, and according to the gradations of the dignities or ranks in this world, or the greatness of their powers, they think they are to be kings and princes, like those earthly monarchs who now exist; chiefly, as it appears, on account of that expression in the Gospel: "Have thou power over five cities." And to speak shortly, according to the manner of things in this life in all similar matters, do they desire the fulfillment of all things looked for in the promises, viz., that what now is should exist again. Such are the views of those who, while believing in Christ, understand the divine Scriptures in a sort of Jewish sense, drawing from them nothing worthy of divine promises.

(*De principiis* II.11.2)

There are three passages from *The Ecclesiastical History (Historia ecclesiastica)* by Eusebius of Caesarea that deserve notice. The portrayal of the kingdom as a future hope[6] can be seen in the winsome account of the appearance of the grandsons of Judas (the brother of Jesus) before Domitian.

The same Domitian gave orders for the execution of those of the family of David and an ancient story goes that some heretics accused the grandsons of Judas (who is said to have been the brother, according to the flesh, of the Savior) saying that they were of the family of David and related to the Christ himself. Hegesippus relates this exactly as follows. "Now there still survived of the family of the Lord grandsons of Judas, who was said to have been his brother according to the flesh, and they were delated as being of the family of David. These the officer brought to Domitian Caesar, for, like Herod he was afraid of the coming of the Christ. He asked them if they were of the house of David and they admitted it. Then he asked them how much property they had, or how much money they controlled, and they said that all they possessed was nine thousand denarii between them, the half belonging to each, and they stated that they did not possess this in money but that it was the valuation of only thirty-nine plethra of ground on which they paid taxes and lived on it by their own work." They then showed him their hands, adducing as testimony of their labour the hardness of their bodies, and the tough skin which had been embossed on their hands from their incessant work. *They were asked concerning the Christ and his kingdom, its nature, origin, and time of appearance, and explained that it was neither of the world nor earthly, but heavenly and angelic, and it would be at the end of the world, when he would come in glory to judge the living and the dead and to reward every man according to his deeds.* At this Domitian did not condemn them at all, but despised

them as simple folk, released them, and decreed an end
to the persecution against the church.

(*Ecclesiastical History* III.19.1–20:5)

Though unfortunate, it is not surprising that in some segments
of the church the concept of a sensory kingdom was given sen-
sual overtones. If the testimony of Eusebius (quoting Gaius)
is trustworthy, this perversion was true of Cerinthus. Though
Cerinthus's conception of the kingdom is invalid, nevertheless
there must have been in the original tradition a sensory concept
of the *basileia* that served as a basis for his perversion.

> We have received the tradition that at the time under
> discussion Cerinthus found another heresy. Gaius, whose
> words I have quoted before, in the inquiry attributed to him
> writes as follows about Cerinthus. "Moreover, Cerinthus,
> who through revelations attributed to the writing of a great
> apostle, lyingly introduces portents to us as though shown
> him by angels, and says that *after the resurrection the kingdom
> of Christ will be on earth* and that humanity living in Jerusa-
> lem will again be the slave of lust and pleasure. He is the
> enemy of the scripture of God and in his desire to deceive
> says that the marriage feast will last a thousand years."
> Dionysius, too, who held the bishopric of the diocese of
> Alexandria in our time, in the second book of his Prom-
> ises makes some remarks about the Apocalypse of John
> as though from ancient tradition and refers to the same
> Cerinthus in these words, "Cerinthus too, who founded
> the Cerinthian heresy named after him, wished to attach
> a name worthy of credit to his own invention, for the doc-
> trine of his teaching was this, *that the kingdom of Christ would
> be on earth,* and being fond of his body and very carnal he
> dreamt of a future according to his own desires, given up to
> the indulgence of the flesh, that is, eating and drinking and
> marrying, and to those things which seem a euphemism
> for these things, feasts and sacrifices and the slaughter of
> victims." (*Ecclesiastical History* III.28.1–5)

The third quotation from Eusebius embodies his discussion of Papias, "a man of very little intelligence, as is clear from his books."

> The same writer adduces other accounts, as though they came to him from unwritten tradition, and some strange parables and teachings of the Savior, and some other more mythical accounts. *Among them he says that there will be a millennium after the resurrection of the dead, when the kingdom of Christ will be set up in material form on this earth.* I suppose that he got these notions by a perverse reading of the apostolic accounts, not realizing that they had spoken mystically and symbolically. For he was a man of very little intelligence, as is clear from his books. But he is responsible for the fact that so many Christian writers after him held the same opinion, relying on his antiquity, for instance Irenaeus and whoever else appears to have held the same views.
>
> (*Ecclesiastical History* III.39.11–13)

From the preceding study of patristic literature[7] two conclusions concerning the kingdom of God are obvious. First of all, in patristic literature (as in the Synoptics) the kingdom was conceived as a *future hope*. Secondly, the kingdom was presented by the church fathers as a spatial phenomenon.[8] Some of them conceived of the kingdom in strictly mundane categories (for example, Irenaeus), while others conceived of it in more "spiritual" terms (for example, Origen). Yet for all the kingdom was a golden age, a coming good time to be experienced in the future by the people of God.

The conception of the kingdom as both a place and a future hope dominated Christian thought until the time of Augustine. Augustine's contribution was the identification of the kingdom with the church.[9]

Notes

1. Outside the Synoptics there are few references in the New Testament to the kingdom of God. This paucity is probably to be explained by the ad hoc nature of much New Testament material. It is easy to understand, for example, why there is no prolonged explication of the *basileia* in a letter like Galatians, which was written specifically to deal with the Judaistic controversy. Verses wherein "kingdom" or "kingdom of God" or "kingdom of Christ" or "kingdom of his beloved Son" occur are John 3:3, 5; 18:36; Acts 1:3, 6; 8:12; 14:22; 19:8; 20:25; 28:23, 31; Rom 14:17; 1 Cor 4:20; 6:9–10; 15:24, 50; Gal 5:21; Eph 5:5; Col 1:13, 4:11; 1 Thess 2:12; 2 Thess 1:5; 2 Tim 4:1, 18; Heb 1:8; 11:33; 12:28; Jas 2:5; 2 Pet 1:11; Rev 1:6, 9; 5:10; 11:15; 12:10; 17:12, 17, 18. Because in these verses the kingdom is not dealt with extensively, it is impossible to use such references to reach a meaningful understanding of the *basileia*. However, as A. E. J. Rawlinson has pointed out in "The Kingdom of God in the Apostolic Age," *Theology* 14 (May 1927): 262–66, in the epistolary literature of the New Testament, the kingdom is thought of as a hope for the future. "How essentially 'eschatological' and 'supernatural' is the Pauline conception of the kingdom is made evident by the brusque statement that 'flesh and blood' (i.e., human nature in its present condition) cannot inherit the kingdom of God" (264).

2. The Tertullian quotations that follow are from A. Cleveland Coxe, ed., *Latin Christianity: Its Founder, Tertullian* (vol. 3 of the *Ante-Nicene Fathers;* ed. Alexander Roberts and James Donaldson; Grand Rapids, Mich.: Eerdmans, 1956).

3. *On Idolatry,* ch. 9; *De Spectaculis,* ch. 30; *On Prescription Against Heretics,* ch. 13; *A Treatise on the Soul,* ch. 55; *Against Marcion* 4.30, 39.

4. *First Principles* II.3.7, II.10.3; *Against Celsus* III.47; V.19.

5. E.g., in *De principiis* II.11.3, Origen agrees that in the kingdom people will eat, but their food will be the "bread of life" that nourishes the soul with "the food of truth and wisdom."

6. F. Edward Cranz, "Kingdom and Polity in Eusebius of Caesarea," *Harvard Theological Review* 65 (January 1952): 47–66. Cranz pointed out in this article that in the thought of Eusebius the destiny of man is the kingdom of heaven, and this destiny is to be realized when Christ comes again.

7. See Hans Bietenhard, "The Millennial Hope in the Early Church," *Scottish Journal of Theology* 6 (March 1953): 12–30, for the citation of additional patristic literature that reveals how the church fathers conceived of the kingdom as a future hope.

8. The initial turning from a concrete to an abstract understanding of the kingdom probably took place in Alexandria under Clement and Origen. Note Origen's interpretation of Luke 17:21 cited by T. W. Manson, *The Mission and Message of Jesus* (New York: E. P. Dutton, 1938), 595. Christian thought, however, has been dominated by the Augustinian equation of the kingdom with the church. An abstract understanding of the kingdom did not become a prominent feature of Christian thought until the nineteenth century.

9. Louis Berkhof pointed out Augustine's identification of the kingdom with the church in his *The Kingdom of God* (Grand Rapids: Eerdmans, 1951). Berkhof's book is a lucid survey of the various concepts of the kingdom of God that have prevailed throughout the history of Christian thought. Attention should also be called to Henry Martyn Herrick's *The Kingdom of God in the Writings of the Fathers* (Chicago: University of Chicago Press, 1903). This is a helpful (though incomplete) guide to the concept of the kingdom in patristic literature.

Appendix C

An Excursus on Luke 17:21

One statement attributed to Jesus is used over and over by theologians who strive to make his kingdom teachings relevant for the Christian faith. That statement is found in Luke 17:21 and asserts, "The kingdom of God is within you." This statement, however, is anomalous when compared to other statements Jesus made concerning the kingdom. Most of his kingdom observations reveal that he thought of the kingdom as a place. In gospel thought people will enter into the kingdom the way they enter into a country or city; the kingdom does not enter or exist within them. Luke 17:21 is the only Jesus statement suggesting the kingdom exists within people. Despite its irregularity, this verse is cited time and again by the clergy when expounding to parishioners what the kingdom of God means. Indeed, Luke 17:21 is the proof text par excellence for interpreters who believe the kingdom is like "peace of mind" or "peace of soul" and is an inward "spiritual" possession of believers.

This inner interpretation, however, is problematic. For one thing, when Jesus made this statement he was talking to Pharisees, members of a Jewish sect devoted to the Torah. They were Jesus' hostile critics. Thus it is difficult to understand why Jesus would have told his critical opponents that the kingdom of God was within them.

To make sense out of Luke 17:21 attention must be given to the context in which it appears. That context is Luke 17:20–37. Jesus and the early church, we now know, believed the historical process was nearing a grand climax. Something startling and magnificent was soon to occur. Would signals or warning signs be given to let people know this climax of history was about to take place?

One tradition in the Gospels suggests Jesus believed warning signs would be given. This tradition is preserved in Mark 13, Matt 24, and Luke 21:5–36. These passages suggest that just before the "end of time" shocking events will take place. Wars, earthquakes, and famines will occur. Jerusalem will be surrounded by armies. The sun will be darkened and stars will fall out of the sky.

But in Luke 17:20–37, the context within which Jesus says, "The kingdom of God is within you," a contradictory view is presented. The main burden of Luke 17:20–37 is a rejection of premonitory signs or apocalyptic timetables as found in Mark 13. Instead, history's denouement will be unexpected and instantaneous. This becomes obvious when it is borne in mind that Luke 17:21 is paralleled by Luke 17:23b–24. These verses can be structurally analyzed as follows:

- *A desire to know the date of arrival*

Being asked by the Pharisees when the kingdom of God was coming, he answered them, "The kingdom of God is not coming with signs to be observed." (v. 20)

And he said to the disciples, "The days are coming when you will desire to see one of the days of the Son of man, and you will not see it." (v. 22)

- *Here or there saying*

. . . nor will they say, "Lo, here it is!" or "There!" (v. 21a)

And they will say to you, "Lo, there!" or "Lo, here!" (v. 23a)

- *Warning of instantaneous arrival*

" . . . for behold, the kingdom of God is within you." (v. 21b)

"Do not go, do not follow them. For as the lightning flashes and lights up the sky from one side to the other, so will the Son of man be in his day." (v. 23b, 24)

(Note the idea of instantaneousness is emphasized by the immediately following illustrations of Noah and the flood and Lot and the destruction of Sodom.)

That Luke 17:21 should be interpreted in terms of Luke 17:24 was recognized years ago by Burton Scott Easton.

> As Lk could not have meant v. 24 to contradict v. 21, the meaning of Christ's answer in Lk's mind is fixed by vv. 22–37: — "The time of the coming of the Kingdom cannot be computed beforehand. When it comes its appearance will be unmistakable, for it will be visible to all." This reply is a condemnation of efforts to determine the time of the end by "jubilees," "world year," etc., or by the appearance of miraculous "signs," a common feature of the current apocalyptic.[1]

Or as T. W. Manson, the English scholar, wrote concerning Luke 17:21,

> We must then understand Jesus to say: The Kingdom does not come in such a way that one can make a programme of its coming. There are no premonitory signs and portents which may be observed so that one could say, "Look at this and that; it cannot be far away now." On the contrary it comes suddenly and unexpectedly. One moment the world is just its normal self: then Lo! the Kingdom of God is among you. This interpretation has two obvious claims to acceptance. It deals with the question asked; and the reply of Jesus agrees with his genuine teaching about the final consummation as given in the passage which follows immediately in Lk. (17:23–30).[2]

In a word, Luke 17:21 does not deal with the kingdom's location. Rather this obscure and anomalous verse deals with the manner of its temporal arrival. Its arrival will be like a flash of lightning! Moreover, this obscure and anomalous verse should not be the hermeneutical touchstone to determine what Jesus meant by the kingdom of God.

Notes

1. Burton Scott Easton, *The Gospel According to St. Luke* (New York: Scribner's, 1926), 261.

2. T. W. Manson, *Mission and Message of Jesus,* 596.

Glossary

Agnosticism. Agnosticism is a term coined by T. H. Huxley, a nineteenth-century English scientist. The word has a Greek etymology and literally means "unknowableness." The term is used in our day to denote the epistemological view that some issues or matters cannot be known. There are limitations to human knowledge. Thus Leslie Weatherhead, a devout English clergyman, could write a book entitled *The Christian Agnostic*. In discussions about the existence or nonexistence of God, the term agnosticism is sometimes confused with atheism: the position there is no God. Agnosticism does not deny God's existence. Instead, agnosticism contends it cannot be known with certainty whether or not God exists.

Anselm, Saint. Saint Anselm (1033–1109 C.E.), born in Asota in northern Italy, was a Benedictine monk who became archbishop of Canterbury in 1093 C.E. He is remembered as a theologian. In a work entitled *Proslogium* he advanced what is now known as the ontological argument for God's existence. His most famous work was entitled *Cur Deus Homo (Why God Became Man)* in which he advanced a "satisfaction" atonement theory contending that Jesus (the God-man) died "to satisfy" God the Father who was offended by mankind's disobedient sinfulness. Hovering in the background of Anselm's thought is the socioeconomic arrangement known as feudalism, a feature of medieval history.

Anthropomorphic. "Anthropomorphic" is composed of two Greek words. One of those words (*anthropos*) means "a human being" or a "person." The other word (*morphe*) means "shape" or "form." Hence "anthropomorphic" means "having the shape or form of a person." One of the oldest beliefs in religion is the belief that God (or the gods) is human in shape. God has a body with a face, arms, and legs. God sits in the sky on a throne and has human emotions like love and anger. A case can be made for the view that the history of religion is a journey from an anthropomorphic view of God to a pantheistic or panentheistic understanding of God.

Apocalyptic Literature. The term "apocalyptic" is based on the first word in the Revelation, the last book in the New Testament. That first word is *apocalypsis,* which means "revelation." Apocalyptic literature is a genre of writings characterized by symbolism and permeated with the belief that world history is on the verge of coming to an end. This "end of time" would involve a divine intervention in human affairs to abolish evil and to establish justice. Daniel in the Old Testament is an example of apocalyptic literature. So is the Revelation in the New Testament. Of help in understanding this type of literature are such works as Norman Cohn's *The Pursuit of the Millennium* (Fairlawn, N.J.: Essential Books, 1957); John Joseph Collins's *The Apocalyptic Imagination: An Introduction to the Jewish Matrix of Christianity* (New York: Crossroad, 1984); Christopher Rowland's *The Open Heaven: A Study of Apocalyptic in Judaism and Early Christianity* (New York: Crossroad, 1982); H. H. Rowley's *The Relevance of Apocalyptic* (New York: Association Press, 1964). Recently published in three volumes is *The Encyclopedia of Apocalypticism* edited by J. J. Collins, B. McGinn, and S. J. Stein, and published by Continuum Press.

Apostolic Fathers. The expression "Apostolic Fathers" should be correlated to the terms "patristic literature" and "patristics." "Patristic literature" and "patristics" are broad terms referring to writings of the church fathers through the eighth century of the Christian era. The expression "Apostolic Fathers" is a narrower term. It refers to the church fathers who wrote *immediately after* the New Testament was written. Thus the Apostolic Fathers are a subcategory of patristic literature. The expression "Apostolic

Fathers" came into use for the first time toward the close of the seventeenth century. These fathers include Clement of Rome, Ignatius, Hermas, Polycarp, Papias, and the authors of such works as the *Epistle of Barnabas* and the *Didache.* Some of these works almost made it into the New Testament. This is particularly true of the *Epistle of Barnabas* and the Shepherd of Hermas. Some of the earliest and most valued manuscripts of the Greek New Testament contain them. Their inclusion shows that for a time the content of the New Testament was fluid. The view of the New Testament as a closed anthology of twenty-seven documents did not crystalize until the last half of the fourth century.

Atonement. "Atonement" (which is not a biblical term) literally means "at-one-ment" ("to make one again"). Reconciliation is a synonym. Across the centuries theologians, relying on the letters of Paul, have constructed "atonement theories." These theories presuppose an estrangement between God and mankind. This estrangement, theologians contend, is due to mankind's sinfulness. Atonement theories suggest God and mankind have been reconciled because of Jesus' sacrificial death. "Substitutionary atonement" is a theory encountered in grassroots Protestantism. This theory contends Jesus was *substituted* on the cross for sinful humanity. "On the cross Jesus took the place of sinners. He suffered for them what they should have suffered." This theory is based on such Pauline statements as "For if while we were enemies we were reconciled to God by the death of his Son, much more, now that we are reconciled, shall we be saved by his life" (Rom 5:10). Or consider 2 Cor 5:20b–21: "We beseech you on behalf of Christ, be reconciled to God. For our sake he made him to be sin who knew no sin, so that in him we might become the righteousness of God." Viewing Jesus' death as a *religious* event (an act bringing about reconciliation between God and mankind) does not harmonize with viewing Jesus' death as a *political* event (the execution of a potential rebel against the Roman Empire). Increasingly atonement theories suffer from a depletion of plausibility.

Augustine. Augustine (354–430) was a philosopher, bishop, and theologian. He was born in Tagaste in an area of north Africa now known as Algeria. He was educated at Tagaste and eventually in Carthage and Rome. As a young man Augustine lived the life of a libertine (fathering a child out of wedlock). For a time he was a Manichaen but eventually became a Christian and bishop of Hippo, a town in north Africa. He died while this town was being besieged by Vandals, barbarian invaders from Europe. Augustine's two major literary works were his *Confessions* and *The City of God.* Augustine identified the kingdom of God with the church. His negative attitude toward sexuality has had a profound influence on Christian thought.

Barth, Karl. Karl Barth (1886–1968) was a Protestant theologian who gained instant fame as a result of his 1919 *Commentary on Romans.* A native of Switzerland who lived for a time in Germany, Barth vigorously opposed Nazism. He left Germany and in 1935 became a theology professor at Basel where he continued to teach until his retirement in 1962. Barth wanted his theology to be biblical in nature and he also wanted theology to return to the principles of the Protestant Reformation. He devoted years of his life to writing his *Kirchliche Dogmatik (Church Dogmatics),* which was his magnum opus.

Basileia. *Basileia* is a Greek word that is translated into English by the word "kingdom." Repeatedly in the Synoptic Gospels the term appears in the phrase *basileia tou theou,* which means "kingdom of God." Etymologically *basileia* is related to the Greek word *basileus,* which means "king." Hence a basilica is a "kingly hall" or an ornate Roman Catholic church building.

Calvin, John. John Calvin (1509–64) was a French church reformer and theologian. Along with Martin Luther and John Knox, he was a major leader of the Protestant Reformation. His break with the Roman Catholic Church took place around 1533 after a religious experience in which he believed he had been charged with the mission of restoring the church to its original purity. He is remembered for writing a systematic theology entitled *Institutes of the Christian Religion,* his exposition of the Christian faith. This work is one of the literary monuments of the Protestant Reformation. Calvin spent much of his adult life in Geneva where he devoted his energies to establishing a theocracy. Austere in his private life, Calvin (unfortunately) was noted for his vindictiveness. Like contemporary fundamentalists, he believed he had the right and duty to decide what was true Christianity.

Decapolis. The word "Decapolis" is Greek, combining the words *deka,* which means "ten" and *polis,* which means "city." The Decapolis ("ten cities") was a confederation of predominantly Gentile cities marked by Hellenistic organization and culture. The Decapolis is mentioned in the New Testament, in Josephus's *Jewish War,* and in the *Natural History* of Pliny the Elder. Scythopolis, which Josephus describes as the greatest Decapolis city, was the only member of the confederation west of the Jordan River. Thus it would be the Decapolis city closest to Nazareth and to Capernaum, the base of Jesus' public ministry.

Deus ex Machina. "Deus ex machina" is a Latin expression meaning "a god from a machine." In ancient Greek and Roman dramas, a god was occasionally introduced by means of a crane to decide the play's final outcome. Thus to think of God or Jesus in terms of deus ex machina means to believe God or Jesus can intervene in human situations to achieve a desired outcome or resolution (particularly in difficult contexts). The deus ex machina belief is similar to the genie-in-a-bottle belief.

Enlightenment. The Enlightenment was a philosophic movement of the eighteenth century marked by a rejection of traditional social, religious, and political ideas and marked also by an emphasis on rationalism. Hence the Enlightenment is frequently referred to as the Age of Reason. The Enlightenment, personified in thinkers like Voltaire, Rousseau, and Thomas Paine, was the first time in which the Christian religion was intellectually challenged in a decisive manner. Earlier thinkers like Celsus (the Voltaire of the second century) had criticized Christianity, but they tended to be lonely and ignored voices in the wilderness.

Epistemology. Epistemology is a major branch of philosophy. Built on the word *episteme,* which is the Greek word for knowledge, epistemology seeks to understand the extent and tools of human knowledge. It struggles with such questions as: How much can we know? What kinds of knowledge exist? What tools do humans possess that enable them to acquire knowledge? Is human knowledge — by its very nature — limited? Some people in our day feel that early Christian theologians did not take seriously the limitations of human knowledge. They were guilty of epistemological inflation.

Eusebius of Caesarea. Eusebius of Caesarea (ca. 260–339 C.E.) was an early, eminent church historian who lived at Caesarea, an ancient seaport south of Haifa on the eastern Mediterranean coast. His major literary work is known as the *Ecclesiastical History.* In this work Eusebius recounts the history of Christianity from the apostolic age down to the time of Constantine, nominally the first Christian emperor of the Roman Empire. His *Ecclesiastical History,* available in paperback from Baker Books of Grand Rapids, Michigan, is indispensable for understanding the opening centuries of the Christian movement.

Fundamentalism. Fundamentalism is a johnny-come-lately in the church's vocabulary. The term appeared initially around the turn of the twentieth century during the struggle over the historical-critical method of biblical studies. Fundamentalism (as used in church history) contends that some beliefs are "fundamental" (or basic) to the Christian religion and under no circumstances should be denied or questioned. Familiar to church historians are the "five points of fundamentalism" hammered out in 1895 at a Bible conference held in Niagara, New York. These five points are the inerrancy of the Bible, the deity of Jesus, the virgin birth, substitutionary atonement, and the second coming of Jesus. Fundamentalists believe their understanding of the Christian faith is right. Christians who disagree with them are deemed heretics. The fundamentalist controversy ravaged churches in the north during the 1930s. The controversy exploded again in the south during closing decades of the twentieth century.

Harnack, Adolf von. Adolf von Harnack (1851–1930) was a famous German church historian and theologian. He was a patristic scholar par excellence. He concentrated on the church fathers (see Apostolic Fathers) who lived before the Council of Nicaea in 325 C.E. He regretted the intrusion of Greek philosophical ideas into Christian theology (an intrusion he labeled as "Hellenization"). He was a prolific writer (publishing, for example, a seven-volume *History of Dogma,* which traced the history of Christian thought down to the time of the Reformation). In the winter of 1899–1900 he delivered a series of famous lectures in which he stressed the moral side of Christianity to the exclusion of the doctrinal side. These lectures were published in English under the title *What Is Christianity?* For decades this book was viewed as a précis of the Christian religion.

Hermeneutics. Hermeneutics (derived from Hermes, the messenger of the gods in Greek mythology) is the art or science of interpretation. Hermeneutics grapples with the question: How is a literary work to be interpreted or understood? Obviously a novel by Ernest Hemingway or a fable by Aesop is not to be interpreted in the same way as a history textbook or a Latin grammar. An enduring question in biblical studies is: How are various parts of the Bible to be understood from a hermeneutical viewpoint? Is the account of the heavenly voice at Jesus' baptism to be understood as the report of an actual event or is the account a pious embellishment? Is the story of Noah's flood a record of an actual event or is it a myth?

Historical-Critical Method. In the eighteenth and nineteenth centuries emerged a new method of biblical study, which today is known as the historical-critical method. At the core of this method was a mutation (a new development) in biblical studies. This mutation can be stated succinctly: Scholars for the first time began studying the Bible as they study other works of literature. When, for example, scholars study Shakespeare's plays, they ask probing questions such as: In which order were the plays written? How does *Hamlet's* structure compare to the structure of *The Merchant of Venice?* Was Shakespeare anti-Semitic? What "message" or commentary on life is conveyed in *Macbeth?* How were the tragedies staged in the Globe Theatre? Shakespearean students make every effort to interpret and to understand the plays in the context of sixteenth- and seventeenth-century English society. During the eighteenth century scholars began using a similar technique while studying the Bible, and this technique (as I have previously observed) came to be known as the historical-critical method — a phrase that is puzzling. Particularly curious is the term *critical* — a word that suggests fault finding. Thus when some people hear about scholars studying the Bible "critically," they — quite understandably — conclude: "Scholars are 'picking' on the Bible. They are searching for faults." But we must remember that the word "critical" has another meaning besides censoriousness. Derived from a Greek root that means "to discern," it also can convey the idea of being *careful, discriminating, exacting.* In this sense we sometimes remark about a person, "He has a cautious, *critical* mind." Or someone remarks, "I need to weigh *critically* all the factors involved before I reach a decision." Or, "We should read newspapers with a *critical eye.*" In these statements "critical" and "critically" have nothing to do with fault finding; instead, they have a connotation of cautiousness. It is in this reflective, cautious sense that "critical" is used in the phrase "historical-critical method." To study the Bible with this method means to examine carefully its books against their historical background (giving attention to when, where, and under what circumstances they were written) and to study them inquisitively as to their text, composition, and character. In other words, the historical-critical method involves the reverent, systematic application of the mind's evaluative and analytical capacities to the books of the Bible.

Hubble, Edwin Powell. Edwin Powell Hubble (1889–1953) was born in Marshville, Missouri, and was educated at the University of Chicago and Oxford. An American astronomer, he demonstrated the existence of galaxies outside our own. By so doing he multiplied immensely the known size of the universe. He also established that the universe is expanding. In 1929 Hubble, who spent most of his professional career at the Mount Wilson Observatory located on a ridge of the San Gabriel Range directly north of Pasadena, California, determined that the more distant a galaxy is, the more rapidly it is receding from our galaxy. This relationship is now known as Hubble's Law. Post-Hubble astronomy's understanding of the vast size and fluid nature of the universe is remarkably different from the Bible's concept of a compact universe.

Incarnation. Incarnation (a word composed of *in* plus *caro,* which is the Latin word for "flesh") is a doctrine that took classical shape during the christological controversies of the fourth and fifth centuries C.E. It is the belief that Jesus as Son of God inherited flesh from his mother (Mary) and that the historical Christ is at once both fully God and fully human. The doctrine was given its classical form at the Council of Chalcedon in 451 C.E. Liberal theologians increasingly question the appropriateness of the incarnation concept for expressing Jesus' salvific significance.

Josephus, Flavius. Flavius Josephus was a Jewish soldier and historian who lived in the first century C.E. He witnessed the

First Jewish Revolt (66 to 70 C.E.) against Rome. This revolt culminated in the destruction of Jerusalem and the Jewish temple. Josephus advocated that Jews recognize the hopelessness of their resistance to Rome. Thus some Jewish thinkers view him as a traitor to the Jewish cause. Josephus is remembered today primarily as an author. His three major works, *Jewish War, Antiquities of the Jews,* and *Against Apion,* were written in Rome, where he lived after the revolt. These works are invaluable to New Testament scholars. They present a picture of life as lived in Palestine of the first century. Without Josephus's writings our knowledge of first-century Jewish life and thought would be considerably diminished.

Kant, Immanuel. Immanuel Kant was born in 1724 in Königsberg in East Prussia on the Baltic Sea. In 1740 he entered the University of Königsberg where he studied in different fields: physics, algebra, geometry, astronomy, logic, and metaphysics. Kant eventually joined the faculty of this university where he taught for some forty years. A bachelor, he was short in stature and frail in health. His daily routine was rigid. Tradition has it that his afternoon walks were regular. He strolled for exactly an hour, eight times up and down the Linden Allee. His daily walk was so punctual that the townspeople set their clocks by it. Kant published difficult-to-read works bearing such titles as *Critique of Pure Reason* and *Critique of Practical Reason.* One of Kant's pivotal insights was a recognition of the severe limitations of human knowledge.

Karma. Karma is a term used in both Hinduism and Buddhism. The term means both "action" and "the consequence of action." Karma contends that every action a person does and every thought and desire a person has shapes or determines that person's next reincarnation or samsara (the view that we live more than one life on earth). Karma is sometimes "explained" in terms of the biblical statement "Whatever a man sows that he will also reap" (Gal 6:7). Karma provides a strong ethical motivation.

Kerygma. Kerygma is a Greek word that means "preaching" or "proclamation" or "message." In New Testament studies and in Christian theology the term refers to the church's proclamation concerning Jesus. The word appears in 1 Cor 1:21 where Paul asserts, "For since, in the wisdom of God, the world did not know God through wisdom, it pleased God through the folly of what we preach (the kerygma) to save those who believe."

Maccabees and 1 Maccabees. The Maccabees were a Jewish family that led a successful revolt (which began in 167 B.C.E.) against Antiochus IV Epiphanes, a Greek king who attempted to destroy Judaism and convert Jews to the worship of Greek gods. An account of this revolt, the first reported revolt in world history waged in the name of religion, is found in a historical work known as 1 Maccabees. 1 Maccabees, written in Greek, is a document in the Septuagint and is included in the Apocrypha.

Mithraism. Mithraism was a prominent mystery religion of the Roman Empire of two millennia ago. It involved a veneration of Mithra, the Indo-Iranian god of light. Mithraism was called a "mystery" religion because its rituals and beliefs were kept secret. Excluding women, it flourished from the second to the fourth centuries in the Roman Empire where it appealed to the working class and particularly to Roman soldiers. Numerous Mithra shrines can be seen today across Europe.

A major Mithra ritual was the taurobolium: the ritual slaying of a bull. The initiate was placed into a pit. On the top of the pit was a lattice-like cover. On this cover a bull was slain. The bull's blood poured down into the pit and the initiate allowed himself to be bathed in the bull's blood. There is also the possibility he drank some of the blood of the slain animal. Having undergone this ceremony, the initiate was endowed with immortality. This kind of thinking may have influenced the Roman Catholic and Eastern Orthodox concept of transubstantiation whereby the wine of the Eucharist becomes the blood of Jesus.

The Mithra scholar par excellence is the late Franz Cumont,

whose research, originally written in French, has been published in English under the title *The Mysteries of Mithra.*

Ontology. "Ontology" is not an easy term to define or to understand. It is based on the Greek words *ontos,* which means "being," and *logos,* which (among other definitions) means "knowledge." Thus ontology means "knowledge of being." The term did not appear in philosophical discourse until the seventeenth century. Wide agreement on what the term precisely means and how it is to be used in theological-philosophical discourse has never existed. In one sense "ontology" means the study of "essence." What is the "essence" or "being" or "inner structure" or "substance" of an apple? Theologians in the past have attempted to understand the "essence" or "being" of Jesus and God. This attempt can be seen in the Councils of Nicaea and Chalcedon. Many contemporary theologians believe this is an impossibility. They believe that humans — because of epistemological limitations — cannot comprehend or know Jesus' or God's "essence" or "being." In the field of psychology (particularly when discussing the issue of perception) "ontology" is used in connection with Locke's distinction between primary and secondary qualities and in connection with Kant's distinction between the noumenal world and the phenomenal world.

Orthodox Christianity. The word "orthodox" is based on two Greek roots: *orth,* which means "right" and *doxa,* which means "opinion." Thus "orthodox Christianity" is that version of the Christian religion which embodies what many deem to be "right opinion" or "right religious beliefs." In this book the phrase is used to designate the understanding of the Christian faith promulgated by the Roman Catholic Church, the Eastern Orthodox Church, and mainline Protestant denominations (like the Methodist or Episcopal Churches.)

Pantheism. Pantheism (from the Greek word *pan,* which means "all" and the Greek word *theos,* which means "God") is the theory that God and the universe are identical. The term was coined in 1705 by J. Toland, a deist. Pantheism is an ideological motif of Hinduism, which views everything as a manifestation of Brahman. It stands in contrast to biblical thought (as found in Gen 1), which distinguishes between God and the created order. *Panentheism* is the belief that the Being of God includes and penetrates the whole universe but (contra pantheism) that God's Being is more than and is not exhausted by the universe. The word was coined by K. C. F. Krause (1781–1832). Paul expressed a panentheistic view when in Athens he quoted Epimenides, "In him (God) we live and move and have our being" (Acts 17:28).

Panentheism. See Pantheism.

Pascal, Blaise. Blaise Pascal (1623–62) was a French mathematician, scientist, and religious writer. To this day he is remembered for his scientific research on the pressure of liquids. At the age of sixteen he wrote a book (now lost) on *The Geometry of Conics,* which attracted the attention of the great mathematician René Descartes, the man frequently described as the father of modern philosophy. Later in life religion became more important to Pascal than his scientific pursuits. He became a monk in a Jansenist monastery. Eight years after Pascal's death his *Pensées* was published; this work was an apology for the Christian religion.

Patristics. Patristics is the area of historical-theological studies dealing with the writings of the Fathers (*patres*) of the church who wrote between the end of the first century (immediately after the composition of the New Testament) down to the close of the eighth century. This period is commonly referred to by church historians as the "Patristic Age." The church fathers were prolific authors. Some representative church fathers are Tertullian, Origen, Augustine, and John of Damascus. Their writings are a gold mine for understanding the way Christians thought and acted during the opening centuries of the Christian movement.

Pentecost. The term "Pentecost" is derived from a Greek word that means fiftieth. It was so named because the Feast of Pentecost is celebrated the fiftieth day after the sixteenth of Nisan, which is the second day of the Feast of Passover. In Judaism this festival is called the Feast of Weeks (*Shavuot*) because it is observed some seven weeks after Passover. Along with the festivals of Passover and Tabernacles, Pentecost was one of the three pilgrim festivals during which Jews visited the temple in Jerusalem. In the idealized history of early Christianity as recorded in the book of Acts, Pentecost was the occasion on which the Holy Spirit descended on the apostolic church. This tradition is in contrast to the tradition recorded in John 20:21 where Jesus endowed his disciples with the Holy Spirit during a resurrection appearance.

Pericope. "Pericope" is a transliteration of *perikope,* a Greek word meaning "section." In church liturgy the term refers to a passage of Scripture to be read in church services. In New Testament studies, however, the term refers to a unit or section of material found in the various gospels. For example, the adultery pericope (John 7:53–8:11) narrates Jesus' compassionate dealing with the women taken in the act of adultery. This pericope is omitted in many ancient manuscripts of the Fourth Gospel. However, the account appears to be an authentic incident in Jesus' ministry, though originally not belonging to John's Gospel. In some Greek manuscripts this pericope is found after Luke 21:38. Scholars recognized years ago that much of the synoptic material (with the exception of the account of Jesus' final week) is comparable to a string of pearls. Just as stringed pearls are independent and unrelated to adjacent pearls, in a similar way many of the synoptic pericopes are self-contained units of Jesus material (or tradition), which probably circulated by word of mouth (the oral tradition) before being written down in the Gospels. Read Mark 4:21–41 and note how verses 21–25 (the lamp pericope) and verses 26–29 (the scattered seed pericope) and verses 30–32 (the mustard seed pericope) and verses 33–34 (the parable pericope) and verses 35–41 (the storm pericope) all are self-contained. They stand by themselves, unrelated to what precedes or follows.

Pilate, Pontius. Pontius Pilate was the Roman governor of Judea from 26 to 36 C.E. He was the Roman bureaucrat who presided over the trial of Jesus and ordered his execution. Some historians view him as a cruel man (Luke 13:1, for example, mentions Pilate mixing the blood of Galileans with their sacrifices). Other historians, noting he remained a governor for a decade, conjecture he was an efficient administrator.

Post-Hubble. See Hubble, Edwin Powell.

Proselyte. "Proselyte" is a transliteration of the Greek word *proselytos,* which means "newcomer" or "visitor." In the New Testament and in rabbinic literature the word is used to designate a Gentile convert to Judaism. The term appears in Matt 23:15 and in Acts 2:10, 6:5, and 13:43.

Rauschenbusch, Walter. Walter Rauschenbusch (1861–1918) can be referred to as the "father of the social gospel." He was born in Rochester, New York. He was graduated from the University of Rochester and in 1886 was graduated from the Rochester Theological Seminary. For several years Rauschenbusch pastored the Second German Baptist Church in the city of New York. This church was located in proximity to a slum section known as Hell's Kitchen. Exposed to Hell's Kitchen, Rauschenbusch witnessed firsthand multiple social ills (inadequate housing, low incomes, inferior medical care). As a result of this slum exposure he was motivated to bring the Christian faith to bear on current social problems. To that end he contended that the kingdom of God must be understood as a just social order. Christians should strive to actualize this kingdom of God on earth. Rauschenbusch advanced his reformist views in such books as *Christianity and the Social Crisis* and *A Theology for the Social Order.*

Sabbath. Sabbath is a term based on the Hebrew verb *shavat,* which means "to rest." Thus the Sabbath is a day of rest, which in Judaism begins on Friday at sunset and lasts until nightfall on Saturday. The Sabbath is connected with God's creation of the world as recounted in Gen 2:2 ("And on the seventh day God finished his work which he had done, and he rested on the seventh day from all his work which he had done"). In Protestant piety the Sabbath (the seventh day of the week) is frequently confused with Sunday (the first day of the week). Early Christians began worshipping on Sunday (the day of the sun) because it was on the first day of the week that Jesus was raised from the dead.

Sacrament. The term "sacrament" translates the Latin word *sacramentum* and the Greek word *mysterion* (which means "mystery"). The Latin *sacramentum* originally meant an oath, especially the soldier's oath of allegiance. In Christian theology and liturgy a sacrament is traditionally defined as "an outward and visible sign of an inward and spiritual grace given to us, ordained by Christ himself, as a means whereby we receive the same." The Councils of Florence (1439) and Trent (1545–63) affirmed seven sacraments: baptism, confirmation, the Eucharist, penance, extreme unction, orders, and matrimony. In Roman Catholic thought the sacraments are viewed as functioning *ex opere operato.* This view contends that a sacrament is an instrument of God and that its effectiveness is not dependent upon the qualities or decency of the person administering the sacrament. Sacraments play a more important role in Roman Catholicism and Eastern Orthodoxy than in Protestantism. In the 1994 *Catechism of the Catholic Church* (in paragraph 1116 on p. 289) the sacraments are described as "the masterworks of God."

Schweitzer, Albert. Albert Schweitzer (1875–1965) was a German theologian, organist, and physician. As an academic he wrote a series of brilliant books, which were translated from German into English. His most famous book (still a classic in biblical studies) was *The Quest of the Historical Jesus*. In this book (and in other books) Schweitzer contended that Jesus was a mistaken prophet who believed the world was about to come to an end. This end of time was to be marked by the arrival of the kingdom of God. Schweitzer gave up an academic career in order to become a medical doctor, spending most of his adult life in French Equatorial Africa caring for the sick. He was an accomplished musician and interpreter of J. S. Bach. Schweitzer was awarded the Nobel Peace Prize in 1953.

Septuagint. Septuagint is a term built on the Latin word for seventy. Seventy is the approximate number of Jewish scholars who in the third and second centuries B.C.E. produced in Alexandria (Egypt) a Greek translation of the Old Testament. Thus in a nutshell: The Septuagint is the Old Testament translated into Greek. This work, parenthetically, has a number of books not found in the Hebrew Old Testament. In biblical scholarship the Septuagint is designated by the Roman numeral LXX. Old Testament quotations in the New Testament are frequently from the Septuagint. The virgin birth tradition in Christianity is based on the Septuagint mistranslation of the Hebrew word *almah* (young woman, not virgin) in Isa 7:14.

Sermon on the Mount. The expression "Sermon on the Mount" is the label given Jesus' discourse ("sermon") recorded in chapters five through seven of Matthew's Gospel. This discourse begins with the Beatitudes and contains such familiar material as the Lord's Prayer and the parable of the two foundations.

Shema. *Shema* is a Hebrew word meaning "hear." In Judaism Shema is the name given to the Jewish confession of faith found in Deut 6:4–9. This confession begins with the assertion: "Hear, O Israel: the Lord our God is one; and you shall love the Lord your God with all your heart, and with all your soul, and with all your might." In our day the Shema is quoted repeatedly in synagogue

services. Jesus quoted the Shema when asked to identify the
greatest of the commandments (Mark 12:28–30).

Son Of Man. Son of Man is a title that is applied to Jesus in
the New Testament. With one exception (Acts 7:56) it is found
only in the Gospels and here always on Jesus' lips. Traditionally
the uses of the term are classified as follows: (1) passages where
clearly it refers to Jesus himself (Matt 11:19), (2) passages where
it refers to the future suffering, death, and resurrection of the
Messiah (Matt 17:22), and (3) passages in which the Son of Man
is to appear at the end of time (Mark 14:62). The interpretation
of the expression is problematical. Did Jesus use the term to
apply to someone *other* than himself? The answer to this question
is not obvious. The expression "Son of Man" may have been
appropriated from the book of Daniel in the Old Testament (see
Dan 7:13).

Substitutionary Atonement. See Atonement.

Synoptics, Synoptic Gospels. The term "synoptic" is composed
of two Greek words that — when combined — mean "to see
together." In New Testament studies the expression "Synoptic
Gospels" (or "Synoptics") refers to the first three gospels in the
New Testament (Matthew, Mark, and Luke) in contradistinction
to the Gospel of John. Matthew, Mark, and Luke present Jesus'
life in a similar way and in a way that is different from the Gospel of John. That the account of Jesus' life found in the Synoptics
is different from the account found in the Gospel of John is a
major conclusion of post-Enlightenment biblical scholarship. For
example, in the Synoptics Jesus' major message is the imminent
arrival of the kingdom of God; in the Gospel of John the kingdom of God is barely mentioned. The Synoptics abound with
parables; the Gospel of John does not contain a single parable.
In the Synoptics Jesus speaks in a telegraphic style; in the Gospel of John he speaks in prolonged discourses. Using metaphors
("I am the door" or "I am the way"), Jesus in the Gospel of

John repeatedly proclaims himself; these egocentric metaphors are missing in the Synoptics. Thus the New Testament contains two fundamentally different presentations of Jesus' life: the synoptic presentation and the presentation of the Gospel of John. New Testament scholars believe the Synoptic Gospels are closer to the historical Jesus than the Gospel of John. This conclusion does not mean that the Gospel of John is void of solid historical details. For example, the Gospel of John does not present Jesus' final meal with his disciples as a Passover meal; the Synoptics — contra historical probability — do present the final meal as a Passover celebration.

Taurobolium. See Mithraism.

Thomas Aquinas. Thomas Aquinas, a Dominican monk, lived his entire life in the thirteenth century (1224–74). Thomas received his education at the Monastery of Monte Cassino, in Paris, and in Cologne. Because he was exceedingly shy and quiet, he was nicknamed the "Dumb Ox" by his fellow students. Thomas eventually became a prolific author. He wrote commentaries on the works of Aristotle and on biblical books. His magnum opus was his *Summa Theologiae,* a summary of theology, in which he sought to interpret the Christian faith in terms of Aristotelian philosophy. In 1879 Pope Leo XIII proclaimed Thomism as the official philosophy of the Roman Catholic Church. Many scholars consider Thomas to be *the* outstanding theologian of the Middle Ages. In many ways he was "liberal" in his views. Tradition contends that toward the end of his life Thomas enjoyed mystical experiences, which made all that he had previously written "seem as straw worthy to be burned."

Torah. *Torah* is a Hebrew word that means "teaching." Unfortunately *Torah* is usually translated into English by the word "law" (hence the "law of Moses" rather than the "teaching of Moses"). Torah is the label Jews give to the first five books of the Old Testament (Genesis, Exodus, Leviticus, Numbers, and Deuteronomy). The term applies to the content (laws, rituals, historical accounts) of these five books. Pious Judaism once believed these books were written by Moses (a view rejected by contemporary scholarship). That there are ten commandments in the law of Moses is a widely held misconception. Jewish scholars contend there are 613 commandments in the Torah.

Theism. Theism is a belief in the existence of a god or gods. "Theism" is derived from *theos,* which is the Greek word for "God" (hence such terms as "theodicy" and "theocracy" and "theology"). Religion makes no sense apart from the conviction that a creative and sustaining power (or powers) exists. In religious language this power or Supreme Being is referred to as "God." Can humans understand or comprehend who or what God is? Many theologians contend we cannot. This epistemological impossibility, however, does not negate God's existence.

Tillich, Paul. Paul Tillich (1886–1965) was a Protestant theologian. A German by birth, son of a Lutheran pastor, Tillich studied at Berlin, Tübingen, and Halle. During the First World War he served as an army chaplain. Because of his connection with the Religious Socialists, he was compelled in 1933 to leave Germany. He came to the United States where he taught successively at Union Theological Seminary in New York, at the Harvard Divinity School in Cambridge, and at the Divinity School of the University of Chicago. Tillich was a prolific writer. Among his better known works are *The Protestant Era, The Shaking of the Foundations, The Courage to Be,* and *A History of Christian Thought.* Probably his most important work was his *Systematic Theology* in three volumes.

Trinity. The Trinity is a central dogma of orthodox Christian theology. The 1994 *Catechism of the Catholic Church* (in paragraph 234 on p. 62) asserts: "The mystery of the Most Holy Trinity is the central mystery of Christian faith and life. It is the mystery of God in himself. It is therefore the source of all the other mysteries of faith.... It is the most fundamental and essential teaching in the 'hierarchy of the truths of faith.'" This doctrine contends that the one God exists in three persons and one substance as Father, Son, and Holy Spirit. God is one, yet self-differentiated. At the Councils of Nicaea and Chalcedon the Trinity doctrine was defined. Scholars like G. W. H. Lampe regard the Trinity belief as outdated.

Troeltsch, Ernst. Ernst Troeltsch (1865–1923) was a German theologian and philosopher. Born in Augsburg, he taught successively at Göttingen, Bonn, Heidelberg, and Berlin. A revealing, laudatory (yet telegraphic) discussion of Troeltsch is found on pp. 526–30 of Paul Tillich's *A History of Christian Thought from Its Judaic and Hellenistic Origins to Existentialism*. According to Tillich, Troeltsch dealt with the relationship between religion and man's mental structure. In this regard he posited the existence of a religious a priori. He denied the possibility of isolating an "essence" of Christianity. Troeltsch argued that the Protestant Reformation of the sixteenth century was essentially a part of the Middle Ages and that the Middle Ages did not end until the Enlightenment. Moreover, he contended that Christianity was mainly a religion for the Western world and not for the Orient.

Vulgate. The Vulgate is a Latin translation of the Bible held in esteem to this day by the Roman Catholic Church. This Latin translation (a monument of Christian scholarship) was produced by Jerome (340–420 Tübingen C.E.), a peripatetic scholar who spent much of his life in Gaul, Rome, Antioch of Syria, and Bethlehem.

Weiss, Johannes. Johannes Weiss (1863–1914) was a German New Testament scholar who for years served as a theology professor at Marburg and Heidelberg. In 1892 he published a small but vastly influential book entitled *Die Predigt Jesu vom Reiche Gottes*. This work has been translated into English under the title *Jesus' Proclamation of the Kingdom of God*. This work was the first prominent attempt in New Testament scholarship to defend the thesis that the central purpose of Jesus' mission was to proclaim the imminent arrival of a utopian kingdom for Jews. That utopian kingdom was the kingdom of God, a topic that dominates the Synoptic Gospels. Weiss was also a pioneer in developing what came to be known later as form criticism (a study of the "forms" that the traditions about Jesus assumed while circulating orally before the writing of the Gospels).

Yom Kippur. Yom Kippur in Hebrew means "day of atonement." This day is described in Lev 16. On this day the high priest wore a plain linen garment and entered the holy of holies (the most sacred place in the Jewish temple) to atone for his own sins and the sins of the entire community of Israel. Two goats were involved in this ceremony. One was sacrificed; the other was driven into the wilderness. Atonement theologians confuse the animal killed at Passover with the animal killed on Yom Kippur. Verses like John 1:29 encourage this confusion.

Scripture Index

General Index